WOMEN IN THE NEW TESTAMENT

WOMEN IN THE NEW TESTAMENT

Questions and Commentary

BONNIE THURSTON

A Crossroad Herder Book
The Crossroad Publishing Company
New York

The Crossroad Publishing Company
370 Lexington Avenue, New York, NY 10017

Copyright © 1998 by Bonnie Thurston

Printed in the United States of America

Library of Congress Cataloging-in-Publication Data

Thurston, Bonnie Bowman
  Women in the New Testament / Bonnie Thurston.
      p.   cm. — (Crossroad companions to the New Testament series)
  Includes bibliographical references.
  ISBN 0-8245-1670-2 (pbk.)
  1. Women in the Bible. 2. Bible. N.T.—Criticism, interpretation, etc. I. Title. II. Series.
  BS2545.W65T48   1998
  225.8'3054—dc21   97-40128
                                                            CIP

1   2   3   4   5   6   7   8   9   10   02   01   00   99   98

In Thanksgiving for

Jane Six Lyle

and

Jane Whitehill Rotch

She opens her mouth with wisdom
and the teaching of kindness is on her tongue.
Proverbs 31:26

Contents

Preface

THE COMPANIONS TO THE NEW TESTAMENT SERIES aims to unite New Testament study with theological concerns in a clear and concise manner. Each volume:

- engages the New Testament text directly;
- focuses on the religious (theological/ethical) content of the New Testament;
- is written out of respect for the integrity of the religious tradition being studied. This means that the New Testament is studied in terms of its own time and place. It is allowed to speak in its own terms, out of its own assumptions, espousing its own values;
- involves cutting-edge research, bringing the results of scholarly discussions to the general reader;
- provides resources for the reader who wishes to enter more deeply into the scholarly discussion.

The contributors to the series are established scholars who have studied and taught the New Testament for many years and who can now reap a wide-ranging harvest from the fruits of their labors. Multiple theological perspectives and denominational identities are represented. Each author is free to address the issues from his or her own social and religious location, within the parameters set for the series.

It is our hope that these small volumes will make some contribution to the recovery of the vision of the New Testament world for our time.

Charles H. Talbert
Baylor University

Acknowledgments

ANUMBER OF PEOPLE have helped and supported me in the preparation of this manuscript. Charles Talbert has again provided constant support and encouragement, wise insight, and helpful suggestions. The editors at Crossroad, especially Robert T. Heller and James Le Grys have been enthusiastic and cooperative throughout the process. George Miller painstakingly reads the page proofs and invariably finds the errors I've missed, for which I am more grateful than he knows. The library at Pittsburgh Theological Seminary is a special joy to me, and Anita Johnson, public service librarian, was wonderful to help me track down obscure books and unlikely periodicals. My colleagues and students at the seminary have tolerated with good humor my occasional "disappearances" to work on the book. To my teachers, colleagues, and students I am especially grateful for encouragement, correction, and stimulation.

My friends have probably suffered most and complained least during the writing of this book. Fr. James O'Brien, S.J., regularly asked about how the work was coming. And my women friends cheer me on in this and all my endeavors. A special thank you to Debra, Kathleen, Lynn, Mary, and Susan.

Finally, I am grateful to the church for its nurture, and especially to the members of the Chapel Hill Christian Church in Brooke County, West Virginia, which was my church family during the writing of this book. God alone knows how much the church and the prayers of the faithful sustain me. I hope this study builds up the church and that any errors of interpretation will be excused as unintentional, for they certainly are.

February 2, 1997
Feast of the Presentation

xi

Abbreviations

1

Introduction

S ETTING OUT TO WRITE ANOTHER BOOK on women and the New Testament strikes me as a little like setting out to take a leisurely
stroll through a mine field. Some of my friends and colleagues
have taken to heart the words of Simone de Beauvoir in *Le deuxième
sexe* that Christian ideology has contributed to the oppression of
women; they have decided that the New Testament is one of the
primary tools of patriarchy and have abandoned it as a source of
authority, direction, or comfort. Others believe that the Bible is the
authoritative word of God and that any discussion of its patriarchal
ethos is at best nonsense and at worst heresy. Wherever I step, something, or somebody, is likely to explode.

Part of the problem, I suspect, is that the subject of women in the
New Testament touches on so many other basic and highly charged
issues, notably language, power, economics, and gender role expectations. Language is probably the human lowest common denominator,
the tool with which we think, communicate with others, and pray.
Language to a large measure determines how we view the world. The
Bible, and most of the great documents of Christianity, was written
when male experience was deemed normative, and thus its language
largely ignores the reality of women's experience. Just how entrenched
that male perspective had become was made apparent in 1980, when
the Division of Education and Ministry of the National Council of
Churches voted to appoint a task force to develop nonsexist translations or paraphrases of readings appointed for use in the three-year lec-
tionary used in many of its member churches. The popular press had a

field day. On November 3, 1980, *U.S. News and World Report* ran an article entitled "Furor Over 'De-Sexing' the Bible," and in the December 8, 1980 edition, *Time* followed suit with "Unmanning the Holy Bible." Language reflects culture. To ask for changes in language is to ask for changes in cultural patterns. One reason it causes so much turmoil is that the quest for inclusive language in the church is as much a cultural as it is a theological or biblical issue.

And so are attitudes toward power. Western societies, which have largely been developed and are certainly run by men, seem to work on the assumption that people prove themselves by performance and achievement, by outdoing others. Mutuality, which stresses each person's intrinsic worth and which insists on cooperation rather than competition, is not highly valued in such a system. The women's movement has pointed up the gap between power (a public virtue) and caring (a private virtue) and has suggested that in the world we now inhabit the power model is outdated. Discussions of women in the New Testament may seem subversive because they point to mutuality and question models of individual and social behavior based on raw power.

Likewise, economics enters into the discussion because economics has largely determined gender roles. In most of the world women's economic sphere is that of unpaid work, housework, child care, subsistence agriculture. In 1983 four-fifths of the world's unpaid work was done by women, who performed two-thirds of the world's work hours but received only 10 percent of the world's income and owned less than one percent of the world's property. As Lisa Leghorn pointed out in the March 1983 *Fellowship* (the magazine of the Fellowship of Reconciliation), the patriarchal golden rule of economics is that he who has the gold makes the rules. In most of the world, men grow up assuming their entitlement to the free work of women.

Closer to home, in the United States, we have moved from an agrarian to a manufacturing and now to a technological economy, from an economy in which the female remained in the home for economic reasons to one in which she often must work outside it to support or help support her family. This working woman encounters an earning capacity well below her male counterparts and what business analysts have called the "glass ceiling." Many women who were sheltered by a husband's presence and income encounter sexual discrimination for the first time when they are forced by divorce or bereavement to enter the labor market. Can the biblical world in which woman's economic value was domestic speak to our situation?

A discussion of gender roles always raises the issue of sexism, any attitude or action that places different values on the nature or activities of men and women because they are or are carried out by men or women. Sexism usually leads to stereotyping, assuming some qualities and activities are ipso facto appropriate to men and some to women and rigidly enforcing the differences (usually in blissful ignorance that such stereotypes are local and culture-specific). Evelyn Scott, a popular novelist of the 1930s, described in her diary the effect of sexual stereotyping. "To have one's individuality completely ignored is like being pushed quite out of life. Like being blown out as one blows out a light." How do first-century A.D. cultural assumptions surrounding gender speak to twentieth-century sexism? Can first-century practice be normative today?

These highly charged general issues not only surround but also subtly influence anything one says about women in the New Testament. And yet they don't even touch on the more emotionally charged theological questions about biblical authority (Whether and how is the Bible a source of authority and a norm for practice?) and ecclesiology (How does the Bible influence the church's practice? Can or should first-century Christianity be replicated in later ages? What is the relationship between church practice and cultural assumption?).

In "The Bible and Feminism," an essay in *Freeing Theology*, Sandra Schneiders makes two points with which few serious New Testament scholars can argue. First, the scriptural record privileges the male as normative and presents females as subject to males by divine design. In short, the Bible is the ultimate patriarchal text and has been used misogynistically throughout its history. And, second, the Bible presents God in primarily (although not exclusively) male terms. (Coarsely put, this in practice has often translated into something like, "since God is male, men are gods.") Simply working toward more accurate translations and understanding more fully the context of the New Testament do not change these fundamental facts.

Frankly, as I thought, studied, and prayed toward the writing of this book, I seriously considered returning my contract to Crossroad Publishing Company with a letter of explanation about the impossibility of the task. But this seemed hypocritical since I preach the New Testament Sunday after Sunday and, in spite of its patriarchal origins, I and my congregations have found it, and the Christ to which it points, liberating. And I recalled what Phyllis Trible wrote in the *Journal of the American Academy of Religion* in 1973, that the "Women's Movement errs when it dismisses the Bible . . . . In rejecting Scripture women ironically accept male chauvinistic interpretations and thereby capitulate to the very view they are protesting" (41/1 [1973]: 31). Yet the dilemma of how to speak meaningfully of the text while treating its context seriously remained.

Just when I was ready to give up in frustration I was asked to review Luise Schottroff's *Lydia's Impatient Sisters* for *Horizons in Biblical Theology,* the journal published by my seminary. In the foreword to that book, Professor Schottroff writes, "Christianity replaced the oppressive patriarchal power over women, men, children, and slaves with a struggle for liberation and the building of just relationships within Christian communities." In a section of her book entitled "Patriarchy and the Hope for the Reign of God," Schottroff traces the patriarchal ideology of domination. In the New Testament *patriarchēs* is used to describe the fathers of the tribes of Israel and the office of bishop. In other ancient writings it refers to the encompassing rule of the father. In Cicero's *De re publica,* for example, the father is the model of direction and guidance. From his rule of the household arises the organization of the state, which is organized like a household. Patriarchy, Schottroff points out, entered Christianity through the church fathers, particularly Augustine. While in the New Testament the Greco-Roman theory of patriarchy is seen most clearly in the household codes (which will be discussed later in this work), Schottroff thinks early Christianity itself participated, as a Jewish liberation movement within the Roman Empire, in an attempt to liberate people from Roman patriarchy.

Schottroff stated clearly that, for her, the most important school of justice is the biblical tradition. Yes, I thought to myself, this is the entrée into the New Testament that both takes seriously its limitations as a historical text and allows the reality of its message to be clearly heard. I can engage myself with the primary task of feminist interpreters (to present the New Testament in ways that neutralize what Sandra Schneiders calls its "oppressive potential" and that invoke what she refers to as "its liberating power . . . on behalf of the victims of church and society") while still remaining firmly within the Christian tradition and community.

In the material that follows I will not be reviewing the literature in the field, which is now vast and complex, although I will make suggestions for further reading. A bibliography of sources and suggestions for further reading follows each major section of the text and is composed primarily of periodical articles on the assumption that standard sources and book-length treatments of the subjects are likely to be both better known and more accessible. I will not be presenting any startlingly new theories or taking serious issue with existing ones, although I hope my acquaintance with the state of the discussions will shed light on the texts presented. First, I attempt to provide a cultural and religious context for the New Testament by briefly outlining the position of women in the Greco-Roman world. Then I shall examine representative New Testament texts presented chronologically by time of composition. That is, we shall look first at Pauline writings as the earliest New Testament witness about women in the early Christian community, and then shall think together about the Gospels, Acts of the Apostles, and Deutero-Pauline texts.

The approach of this study will be to try to ferret out ways in which early Christianity attempted to liberate people from oppression (particularly patriarchy) and to point out the places and ways in which the early Christian community compromised with the dominant society and why that might have taken place. In an article in *Semeia* (vol. 47), "Can an Enslaved God Liberate? Hermeneutical Reflections on Philippians 2:6–11," Sheila Briggs points out that, with regard to liberation, three kinds of New Testament texts exist: texts in which the voice of the oppressed is heard; texts that present the convictions, values, and interests of the dominant society; and texts that are ambiguous. Throughout this work, I make explicit which sort of text is being discussed. The reader will gain the most from this book by reading the biblical text before reading my commentary on it and by leaving the Bible open in order to consult the text to confirm or to challenge my assertions.

Practically speaking, when dealing with biblical passages I will begin with the text itself, with traditional textual analysis and careful translation. Then the passage is discussed in its literary and cultural context, in hopes of discovering something of what was being communicated to the original audience, and why. A primary question asked of each text will be, Who benefits from the telling of this story or the transmission of this tradition? In this regard the "hermeneutics of suspicion" discussed and masterfully practiced by Elisabeth Schüssler Fiorenza is invaluable. And so is listening to the silences, noting what is not said. Only finally will the discussion move toward proclamation, suggestion of the text's meaning for today. Since my first scholarly training was in literature, it is not surprising that I find the New Testament text more like poetry than like scientific writing. I assume that no text has one correct meaning (although some interpretations can be demonstrated to be more correct than others). Multivalence is one of the riches of poetry and sacred writings. Since the real meaning of the text resides in part in the interaction between it and the reader, the author and his or her original intention do not completely circumscribe meaning, although the original intention is to be taken seriously when it can be determined. Finally, I treat the New Testament respectfully as the sacred literature it is.

The final motive of this book is probably pastoral, to suggest that with regard to women early Christianity was a movement of liberation, that the God of the New Testament revealed in Jesus Christ is the God of Hebrew scripture, a God of justice, a God with an ear especially turned toward the oppressed and disenfranchised. That cultures and societies presented or described God in male or patriarchal terms does not make God male or patriarchal. As I understand it, the New Testament is the literary record of God's most dramatic attempt to be better known by human beings. If the writers of the New Testament in some ways fell short of God's self-revelation, it is not God's fault. The Word, after all, became flesh, not book.

And here the mine field begins. Walk carefully with me. Watch where you stand. I invite you to listen for explosions and to examine why they went off in you.

For Further Reading

Women and Religion Generally

Belenky, Mary Field, et al. *Women's Ways of Knowing.* New York: HarperCollins, 1986.

Carr, Anne E. *Transforming Grace: Christian Tradition and Women's Experience.* San Francisco: Harper & Row, 1988.

Christ, Carol P., and Judith Plaskow, eds. *Womanspirit Rising: A Feminist Reader in Religion.* San Francisco: Harper & Row, 1979.

Daly, Mary. *Beyond God the Father.* Boston: Beacon, 1973.

Gilligan, Carol. *In a Different Voice: Psychological Theory and Women's Development.* Cambridge, Mass.: Harvard University Press, 1982.

LaCugna, Catherine Mowry, ed. *Freeing Theology: The Essentials of Theology in Feminist Perspective.* San Francisco: HarperSanFrancisco, 1993.

MacHaffie, Barbara J. *Her Story: Women in Christian Tradition.* Philadelphia: Fortress, 1986.

Mollenkott, Virginia Ramey. *The Divine Feminine: The Biblical Imagery of God as Female.* New York: Crossroad, 1987.

Murphy, Cullen. "Women and the Bible." *Atlantic Monthly* 272/2 (August 1993): 39–64.

Ruether, Rosemary R., ed. *Religion and Sexism.* New York: Simon & Schuster, 1974.

Schneiders, Sandra M. *Beyond Patching: Faith and Feminism in the Catholic Church.* New York: Paulist, 1991.

Trible, Phyllis. *God and the Rhetoric of Sexuality.* Philadelphia: Fortress, 1978.

Feminist Biblical Interpretation

Collins, Adela Yarbro, ed. *Feminist Perspectives on Biblical Scholarship.* Chico, Calif.: Scholars Press, 1985.

Russell, Letty M., ed. *Feminist Interpretation of the Bible.* Westminster, 1985.

_____, ed. *The Liberating Word: A Guide to NonSexist Interpretation of the Bible.* Philadelphia: Westminster, 1976.

Schneiders, Sandra M. *Women and the Word.* New York: Paulist, 1986.

_____. *The Revelatory Text: Interpreting The New Testament as Sacred Scripture.* San Francisco: HarperSanFrancisco, 1991.

Schottroff, Luise. *Lydia's Impatient Sisters: A Feminist Social History of Early Christianity.* Louisville: Westminster/John Knox, 1995.

Schüssler Fiorenza, Elisabeth. *Bread Not Stone: The Challenge of Feminist Biblical Interpretation.* Boston: Beacon, 1984.

_____. *But She Said.* Boston: Beacon, 1992.

_____. *Jesus Miriam's Child, Sophia's Prophet: Critical Issues in Feminist Christology.* New York: Continuum, 1995.

_____. *In Memory of Her: A Feminist Theological Reconstruction of Christian Origins.* New York: Crossroad, 1983.

———, ed. *Searching the Scriptures.* 2 volumes. New York: Crossroad, 1993, 1994.

2

Cultural and Religious Backgrounds

SINCE PART OF THE THESIS OF THIS BOOK is that Christianity was, among other things, a movement for liberation in an oppressive society, it is important to know something of the cultural and religious situation of women in the areas from which the religion sprang and in which it first appeared and subsequently flourished. The following material is presented in very general terms. It is an attempt to give the lay of the land with regard to women and not a more general introduction to the period or a carefully drawn map of anything in the landscape. (For more detailed and comprehensive information, the reader is referred to Ernest Barker's *From Alexander to Constantine;* William Tarn and G. T. Griffith's *Hellenistic Civilization;* the three volumes of M. Rostovtzeff's *Social and Economic History of the Hellenistic World;* and especially the twelve volumes of *The Cambridge Ancient History,* and to the bibliographies provided.)

In feminist reconstructions of history, methodology is crucial. It is important that women, and not male attitudes about women, be central. The task is complicated because the sources are both limited and, when they exist, often presented from the male perspective. Because source material is limited, it is important to use all the types of materials available, inscriptions, monuments, papyri, pictorial evidence, and material remains as well as literary documents. When using literary documents we must take care to discern their perspective. For example, statements about women made by rabbis in the Mishnah may represent their view of women and their prescriptions with regard to them, not the reality of women's lives. Documents may appear to be descriptive when, in fact, they are prescriptive.

8

Furthermore, as feminist scholarship has pointed out, the customarily drawn lines between groups (Jewish women as opposed to Hellenistic women, Jewish women as opposed to Christian women) are not necessarily accurate. Jewish women in the New Testament period lived in the Greco-Roman world; their culture as Jewish women was already deeply influenced by Hellenism. Likewise, Christian women were frequently Jewish women. (Recall the origins of the mother of Jesus, Mary and Martha of Bethany, or Lydia.) In short, the business even of describing the condition and world of women in the New Testament period is a good deal more complex than many have assumed. Nevertheless, in an introductory study such as this one, context is essential, and I offer the following material in full knowledge that it is partial and biased by my own presuppositions.

Before Abraham

It is important to begin by noting that in the most ancient human communities of which there is record, God was thought of in female terms. When we examine the concept of God in primitive societies, we are dealing in the realm of mythology. Myths arise to answer questions about how things came to be as they are. Contrary to popular connotations of the word "myth" as synonymous with "falsehood," myths are the most true stories that exist. (A fine discussion of this point is William J. O'Malley's article, "The Quest for a Myth," *America* [November 23, 1996]:18–21.) Rudolf Otto, in his classic study *The Idea of the Holy*, suggests that the origin of mythology is an apprehension of the numinous. People experience a mysterious power or force and go about trying to describe that experience.

Mythology greatly affects the societies in which it arises. Myths determine how people think about the world; they condition people to think in certain ways. Myths portray actions that are rewarded or punished and thus teach which behaviors are to be emulated and which are to be avoided. From myths we learn what was acceptable in the societies from which they came. Not surprisingly, the myths that grew from societies that thought of the deity as female provided very different images of womanhood from those offered by the male deities of Western monotheism.

Monotheism with a male deity is a latecomer on the stage of human history. Archaeologists have traced the worship of the goddess to

Neolithic communities of 7000 B.C., and some argue that the form goes back to Upper Paleolithic times, 25,000 B.C. Human religion during the long years of stone-age culture was the cult of the mother goddess. It is thought that societies were matrilineal (inheritance passed through the female line) and matriarchal (women in family and public positions of power). It is a chicken-and-egg question whether the sex of the deities determined the sex of the rulers or vice versa. (And, as we shall see, a female god did not necessarily translate into improved circumstances for mortal women.) In any case, goddess religion was subdued by patriarchal nomadic warriors who dominated the Mediterranean in the second millennium B.C. (roughly the time of Abraham). They replaced the earthy mother goddess with a sky god, and from the eighth century B.C. to the seventh century A.D. monotheistic, patriarchal religious reform worked to suppress goddess religions.

These are the broad historical facts. Such developments encompassed thousands of years longer than the time from the birth of Jesus of Nazareth to the present. There were, in fact, roughly three stages in the development of religions with a female god. First, the female goddess reigned supreme. She created and ruled alone without the help of a consort. Next, the goddess is supposed to have shared her rule with a brother/husband or son/husband. Finally, some form of ritual intercourse between the goddess and a male figure was instituted to ensure fertility of the land.

The cult of the supreme mother goddess developed before coitus was associated with childbirth, when the female was believed to be the sole giver of life. The life-producing mother symbolized fertility, so the veneration of maternity as a divine principle emerged. Although it has come down to us very sketchily, the mythology of the time emphasized the "world egg" as a sort of womb from which all grew. The first figures that have been found which are associated with this cult date from the seventh millennium B.C. and emphasize the breasts, navel, hips, and vulva of the female. Many of these figurines are squatting, the birth position in the ancient Near East.

Something of the nature of the worship of the sole mother goddess is captured in this ancient Indian hymn:

> O Mother! Cause and Mother of the world!
> Thou are the One Primordial Being,
> Mother of innumerable creatures,
> Creatrix of the very gods . . .
> O Mother, in hymning Thy praise I purify my speech.

Development of the mother goddess religions was tied to the transition from food gathering to agriculture. Gradually, the birth cult was brought into relationship with the seasonal cycle, and the goddess became associated with the generative powers in nature, and was, therefore, responsible for periodic renewal of life. With the domestication of animals and the beginnings of a rudimentary animal husbandry, males became more religiously important.

Since the source of all life was the woman/goddess, the god too was understood to descend from her; he was both her son and her husband. Eventually the female was associated with procreation in perpetuity, the male with the changing of the cosmic cycles. Every year the summer vegetation was overcome by the power of death. The god, who represented vegetation, sank down into the underworld, and the mother goddess went down to defeat the powers of death, usually by gathering up the scattered pieces of the god's body. She resurrected him from the dead, and he took the throne in a renewed world. This enthronement was celebrated by a sacred marriage.

The Babylonian version of this pattern has Ishtar going to the netherworld to get Tammuz. All is barren while she is gone, but after removing all her clothes bit by bit at the various gates of hell she rises triumphant. A similar pattern is played out in the Isis/Osiris and the Venus/Adonis myths. In each the goddess is not a passive figure but the active agent in the drama of the renewal of life. She was warrior, virgin, and mother, ever-fertile, never old; she preserved her autonomy and was immortalized in hymns like this prayer to Ishtar:

> I pray to thee, O Lady of ladies, goddess of goddesses,
> O Ishtar, queen of all peoples, who guides mankind aright.
> O supporter of arms, who determines battle,
> O possessor of all divine power, who wears the crown of dominion,
> O Lady, glorious is thy greatness; over all the gods it is exalted.

As animal husbandry became more a matter of domestic routine, the goddess cults changed again. The goddess and the god/king underwent a ritual marriage to ensure the fertility of the land. The king and queen (or temple personnel) engaged in ritual sexual union as "stand-ins" for the gods. Generally the king and a priestess enacted the myth which symbolized the god's death and resurrection, followed by his reunion with the goddess. This sacred marriage ensured the reproductive forces of nature after the winter. A feast followed in which the whole population enjoyed the abundance now assured by the completion of the rite. Such rites could, and did, become orgiastic. The Greeks and later the Romans particularly disapproved of them but could do little to stop them because of their enormous popular appeal.

One final development in the history of god-as-female should be noted. The mythology of classical Greece (500–400 B.C.), evinces a distinct hostility to the goddess. There were individual goddesses like Artemis the huntress, Athena the warrior maiden, Aphrodite the goddess of love, and Hera the mother-wife, but the most dignified of these were virgins. The ancient symbol of woman as mother was blocked out, and sexuality and maternity became inferior powers. The female as symbol was split into a lower biological and a higher spiritual function, and only the goddess-as-virgin was extolled. This mirrors both the dualism of classical philosophy and the socially and politically inferior position of the wife in classical Greece. And, as we shall see, this emphasis on virginity was transferred into early Christianity by those of her theologians who were classically trained.

To summarize, the rise of goddess worship and a female kinship system were closely entwined in the ancient Near East. Veneration of a goddess and matrilineal descent of name and property were closely related. There was a gradual shift from the goddess as sole creator, to goddess with a male consort, to the goddess as secondary and/or virginal. Apparently the matriarchal systems were resented by the patriarchal invaders, who began to arrive about 2400 B.C. in the historical records. From that time until 500 A.D., when the last of the goddess temples were destroyed, the religious history of the west became increasingly patriarchal.

The transition of the Hebrew peoples from seminomadic herders to sedentary farmers provides a case in point of the religious struggles in the Fertile Crescent. Their sky god, the patriarchal Yahweh, had been a God of wanderers, unlike many ancient gods, not tied to geography or a specific nation. But the Hebrews' relationship in Canaan was to the soil and to the whole natural sphere to which the farmer was bound. Baalism, the religion native to the area, was a practical religion for farmers and attractive to the Hebrews who knew little of farming or agricultural life. Yahweh had demonstrated that he could control and work in historical circumstances. Just as Yahweh had battled the gods of Egypt (Exodus 7–12), now in Canaan he was placed in the position of having to "win out" in a rivalry with the goddesses of nature religions (see Judg. 2:13; 10:6; and 1 Sam. 7:4 and 12:10, for example).

The matter came to a head, of course, because Yahweh was a jealous God who would not share his absolute sovereignty. His lordship was absolute. Joshua's appeal at Shechem, "choose this day whom you will serve" (Josh. 24:15), was an either-or choice involving no compromises. While the religion of Baal/Ashtarte taught worshipers to control the gods by ritual enactments, the Hebrew faith stressed serving God by absolute obedience to divine commands. No syncretism was to be tolerated. While the first serious conflicts with goddess cults took place during the period of the judges (ca. 1200–1020 B.C.), it took centuries for their cultural influence to be stamped out of what later came to be Judaism. And vestiges of this struggle, and even the *magna mater* religions of the Roman Empire, influenced the development of early Christianity and are reflected in the New Testament.

BIBLIOGRAPHY

Bakan, David. *And They Took Themselves Wives: The Emergence of Patriarchy in Western Civilization*. New York: Harper & Row, 1979.

Campbell, Joseph. *The Masks of God: Oriental Mythology*. Baltimore: Penguin, 1962.

Hooke, S. H. *Middle Eastern Mythology*. Baltimore: Penguin, 1963.

James, E. O. *The Ancient Gods*. New York: Putnam, 1960.

Neumann, Eric. *The Great Mother: An Analysis of an Archetype*. New York: Pantheon Books, 1955.

Olsen, C., ed. *An Introduction to the Mother Goddess and Her Cult* New York: Crossroad, 1982.

Stone, Merlin. *When God Was a Woman*. New York: Harcourt, Brace, Jovanovich, 1978.

JUDAISMS

As Jacob Neusner has taught us, it is more accurate to refer to "Judaisms" than to "Judaism," since apparently at no point in its history was Judaism monolithic, and this is so of the biblical period, especially of the Second Temple. In the time of the judges the Hebrews practiced their religion differently according to the cultic shrines visited. The building of the First Temple during the united monarchy was, in part, an attempt to centralize and standardize the religion, but with the division of the kingdoms Hebrew religion was split into a northern branch (which looked back to the traditions of Moses and the Exodus as paradigmatic) and a southern branch (which saw Davidic kingship as the golden age). With the exile Yahwism was practiced both by those who remained in Palestine and by the exiles in Babylon, where astral religions and Babylonian thought came to exert an influence upon it. The building of the Second Temple at the return and the covenant renewal under Ezra were, again, intended in part to unify Judaism. But when Israel came under the influence of Hellenism, and later under the domination of the Roman Empire, major changes in theology and praxis ensued. Apparently, while both groups were Jews, Jews in Palestine and Jews in the Diaspora were culturally very different.

The Judaisms of the New Testament period were, effectively, Hellenistic Judaisms, Judaisms that had been influenced by the cultural program of Alexander and the philosophy of the Greeks. The Judaisms of the time of Jesus and the New Testament period might well be discussed simply as one of the many Greco-Roman religions practiced during the time. But because Hebrew scripture and Jewish belief and practice so influenced nascent Christianity, it is treated separately here. (Because the sources overlap, the bibliography for Judaism and Greco-Roman society are presented together at the end of the chapter.)

The images of women in Hebrew society have much in common with what is known of the lives of women in the ancient Near East; the traditional view is that women's "place" was domestic and maternal. What Joachim Jeremias calls the *patria potestas* exerted great power over women. Up to the age of twelve and a half, a father had absolute power over his daughter. (For specific examples of this, see the story Lot's daughters in Gen. 19:4–8 or of Jephtha's daughter in Judg. 11:29–40.) He could require her to marry his choice of husband or he could sell her into slavery. After twelve and a half, she could not be betrothed against her will, but betrothals were often contracted early. With the betrothal ceremony the power of the father began to be transferred to the husband, and marriage signaled the "acquisition" of the woman by the man.

A husband was required to support his wife, to provide her food and clothing, to fulfill what Jeremias delicately calls his "connubial duty," and to redeem her in case of captivity or provide for her funeral if she died. The wife's duties were domestic: to wash. cook, care for children, tend the home, spin and weave, and provide for her husband's needs (including washing his face, hands, and feet). The wife was obliged to obey her husband as master, and anything she found as well as any money she earned belonged to him. That polygamy was permissible and that only a husband could sue for divorce indicate the status of a wife vis-à-vis her husband.

Religiously, the Jewish woman was secondary to her husband. Only he was fully a member of the covenant community (as the rite of circumcision made clear). The Torah was binding only on free adult males. While the woman was subject to all the prohibitions of the Torah, according to rabbinic tradition only three were binding on her: the lighting of the Sabbath candles, burning a small piece of dough prior to baking bread, and observing Niddah, laws of menstrual purity. The Jewish priesthood was strictly restricted to men. Generally speaking, women were not included in study of Torah. They were excluded from all of the Temple precincts except the Court of the Women. They were not permitted to bear witness in religious court. Women were linked with slaves and children in their inferior status.

Rabbinic literature not only views women as inferior to men; it sometimes treats them as contemptible. The infamous prayer "Praised be God that he has not created me a gentile; praised be God that he has not created me a woman" and the injunction "Rather should the words of the Torah be burned than to be entrusted to a woman" are but two examples of the attitudes toward women. Like all her Semitic sisters, officially the Jewish woman was chiefly valued for her fertility and for the production of sons. Her primary spheres of activity were domestic, reproductive, and nurturing, caring for husband, household, and children.

In the Essene community centered at Qumran, but with adherents throughout Palestine, women were especially limited. Apparently the community at Qumran was entirely male (Only male skeletons have been found in the community cemetery. Bones of some women and children were found in a peripheral area and are believed to be of those who died there during the annual gathering of the sect.) The recently published *Temple Scroll* notes that women and proselytes were to enter only the Temple's outer court; menstruating women were to be barred from Jerusalem altogether. Sexual regulations in the document are primarily binding on women, and no leadership roles for women are tolerated.

The ethnographic fieldwork of archaeologist Carol L. Myers has broadened considerably our understanding of women's lives in Israelite villages and consequently our understanding of women in the Judaisms of the period. Probably 90 percent of women in the biblical period lived in farming villages in Palestine. The family household, which included several generations and retainers, was an economic as well as a social unit. Families provided for themselves by growing grain, olives, and grapes and by keeping domestic animals. Women's work in this family economy included working in the fields, preserving foodstuffs, preparation of food, routine care of domestic animals, and making of clothing (which included shearing wool, carding, spinning, weaving, and sewing).

Myers has noted both the great time expenditure involved in these tasks and the degree of technological expertise and managerial ability involved. She argues that female labor was no less valuable than male, so daughters would, in fact, have been welcome. In urban areas where husbands were not farmers, women would not have played an essential economic role, and thus their value in society would have been lower. This is an important point, since much of our literary evidence about women's lives comes from urban settings. High infant mortality rates (as many as half the children born died before adulthood) and the dangers of pregnancy may have accounted for the short life span of women, which is thought to have been about thirty years. (Men lived only ten years longer on average.) Myers also believes that women played prominent roles in domestic religious practice, local festivals, and funerary rites.

It is true that in Hebrew scripture there are two distinct "mythologies" concerning women. In the pre-fall tradition, woman was the last stage in the process of creation; she brought to perfection what was imperfect. In the second, post-fall tradition, woman is understood as the temptress who caused the fall. Her moral inferiority results in her inferior status vis-à-vis men. Unfortunately, the latter, misogynistic view predominates in the law.

This is not to say that Hebrew scripture does not have examples of extraordinary women who were greatly valued and respected. Three women are positively referred to as "prophets," Miriam (Exod. 15:20–21), Deborah (Judg. 4:4–6), and Huldah (2 Kgs. 22:14–20). Ruth acted independently to support herself and her mother-in-law. Esther is celebrated for using her beauty and wits to save her people. And the Hasmonean dynasty had queens as well as kings. Nor is Hebrew scripture without positive images of women. Proverbs 31 praises the skill and productivity of a good wife. Recent scholarship has noted that the Song of Solomon shows remarkable mutuality in its view of sexual love. In fact, the woman has the majority of the dialogue in that book and initiates as well as accepts love making.

Nor should it be overlooked that God is occasionally described by using female imagery. Moses depicts God in maternal images as wet nurse (Num. 11:12) and birth-giver (Deut. 32:18). Hosea describes God feeding a child, teaching it to walk, healing its wounds, in short, behaving as its mother. In several passages in Isaiah God is described in terms of giving birth (42:14; 46:3–4). Proverbs and the later wisdom literature reflect the feminine figure of Wisdom, who was present with God when the world was created. Wisdom is, in many ways, the feminine side of Israel's God. While modern feminist readings of Hebrew scripture find these feminine images of God encouraging (as, indeed, they are), they may well reflect the enduring tendency to worship the goddess as well as Yahweh; they may be a way that earlier religious mythology was made acceptable and woven into the later, dominantly patriarchal pattern.

All scholars working to reconstruct earlier periods of history struggle with problems connected with sources. The issue of sources for our understanding of women in Judaism in the New Testament period is especially complex. Ross Kraemer has noted the great disparity between rabbinic sources (the earliest of which is the Mishnah, a collection of discussions about points of Jewish law) and the information provided by epigraphical, archaeological, and nonrabbinic writings. Rabbinic writings led many scholars (like Joachim Jeremias, whose work I used at the beginning of this section) to assume that Jewish women led circumscribed lives of exclusion from much of the religious life of Judaism. But evidence from the Greco-Roman world gives another picture.

The rabbis taught that women were subject to the three binding precepts mentioned above. They are exempt from studying the Torah. The rabbis saw women almost exclusively as sex objects and sources of danger, social disruption, and temptation. The Mishnah not only excludes woman from leadership in the community; it suggests she has no capacity for it. In fact, women are largely ignored in the Mishnah so long as they fulfill their expected roles. Only when they "step outside the boundaries" are they addressed. Prescriptions against women are apparently a response to their attempts at autonomy and authority. In short, in rabbinic sources women are "beyond the pale."

But the picture that emerges of the lives of Jewish women in the

Greco-Roman Diaspora can be very different, indeed. For example, rabbinic sources suggest that women were seated separately from men in the synagogues. But no archaeological evidence confirms this. Bernadette Brooten's book *Women Leaders in the Ancient Synagogue* has done ground-breaking work in the field of inscriptions. According to her findings women were not only prominent as financial supporters of synagogues (especially in Roman Asia Minor) but they held positions as heads of synagogues (Rufina of Smyrna in the second century, Theopempte of Myndos in the fourth) and as elders. (Women elders are attested in Thrace, North Africa, and Malta.) Brooten argues convincingly that these titles were not honorific, but that women performed the same duties as men with identical titles. And women are attested also as "mothers" of specific synagogues, which probably meant they made significant financial contributions to them. It has long been known from Philo's writings that among the Therapeutics (a Jewish monastic community outside Alexandria) both men and women interpreted scripture and participated in rites and festivals.

Ross Kraemer is probably correct when she suggests that the Greco-Roman world, especially Asia Minor (the locus of Pauline Christianity), was more open to the leadership of women in public life, especially in spheres in which civic and religious responsibility intersected. It is certainly the case that the situation of women in the period's Judaisms was much more complicated and more interesting than a simple generalization such as "women were second-class citizens in first-century Judaism" would initially lead one to think.

HELLENISM/GRECO-ROMAN WORLD

By "Hellenism" I mean geographically the "Greco-Roman world," the territory from Greece to the Indus River that came under the sway of Alexander the Great. That empire was the basis of the Roman Empire, which stretched from Britain through Asia Minor, from Gaul to North Africa. "Hellenism" is also a short-hand way of referring to the whole cultural program of Alexander, who not only expanded his empire geographically, but exported its language, culture, religions, and life-style.

As was the case with Judaism, there is great diversity in the lives of women in the Hellenistic and Greco-Roman worlds. Those empires were huge and brought with them both geographic and ethnic diversity. But then, as now, economic status was most determinative in shaping the choices open to women. As was the case in our discussion of Judaisms, there is no monolithic social pattern, no one picture of the role of women in Greco-Roman society that emerges as normative. What follows here is, first, a look at Hellenistic women, then women under Roman law, and finally an introduction to several of the religious options open to women in the empire.

Hellenistic Women

Public records provide more information on Hellenistic women than is available on Greek women in earlier times. This in itself suggests that the position of women was changing. In the classical period, Athenian women did not participate in public affairs or politics but remained at home and raised legitimate children for their husbands. When Philip II took the throne of Macedon in 359 B.C., the independence of the city-states effectively came to an end, and many changes, including in the roles of women, ensued. Among Macedonian ruling classes, the relationships between mothers and sons was strong and exerted powerful influence on society. Many of the Macedonian queens were ambitious, shrewd, and ruthless. For example, Olympias, the mother of Alexander the Great, supported his cause against rival wives and mistresses of Philip II, and when Alexander was away on military campaigns, she presided over the Macedonian court.

The prestige and influence of the queens were emulated by aristocratic women. Public decrees honoring women for public service occur with increasing frequency during the Hellenistic period. Because of their economic and cultural prowess Hellenistic women were occasionally granted citizenship and political rights. Aristodama, a poetess of Smyrna, was granted honorary citizenship by the Aetolians. In the first century B.C. one Phile of Priene was a female magistrate and a second-century B.C. inscription notes the existence of a female magistrate in Histria. In short, as women acquired wealth, they exerted economic power and thereby became more publicly and politically prominent.

In areas hellenized through conquest (as opposed to the old cities of Greece) the legal status of women improved relatively rapidly. Egyptian documents, for example, show women as buyers, sellers, lessors, lessees, lenders, and liable for taxes, as well as able to receive and make legacies. Married women's rights also expanded during the period. The role of a bride's father diminished and the rights of married daughters to be free from paternal authority increased. Marriages were usually arranged for women by their fathers or other male relatives. Divorce became increasingly easy; marriage contracts begin to show evidence that either the husband or wife could repudiate the other, and divorced women were frequently able to keep their dowries. Widows or divorced women who remarried had a greater element of choice in their second husbands, but young widows were expected to remarry.

As the position of women improved in some parts of the Hellenistic world, there was an almost predictable backlash in Greece and specifically in Athens. Under the rule of Demetrius of Phalerum (317 to 307 B.C.) a board of "regulators of women" (*gynaikonomoi*) was established in Athens to censor women's conduct and to control their dinner parties! Stoicism, the most popular of the Hellenistic philosophies (which later exerted considerable influence on the Romans) encouraged traditional roles for women. Because of its influence, the Romans came to regard marriage and bearing children as a moral and patriotic duty. The Neopythagoreans wrote several treatises on the proper behavior of women, "proper" meaning "traditional."

On the other hand, Epicurus admitted women to his school along with men. There is evidence that physical education became available to wealthier women, although they did not participate in the games until well into the first century A.D. Increasing literacy for women is attested by the existence of female poets like Erinna of Telos. In Hellenistic Egypt it is believed that more women than men could sign their names. But it was the courtesans who were probably the most highly educated, sophisticated, and notorious women of the period. Courtesans like Aspasia (the companion of Pericles), Thais (the companion of Alexander), and Phryne (friend of Hyperides) had very different and much more liberated lives than the common prostitutes who were frequently slave women who had been rescued from death by exposure and became sources of income for their owners.

This fact recalls the marked gap between the wealthy and the poor. Wealthier women had more choices and opportunities than did their impoverished sisters, although women living in cities were more restricted than rural women, who needed to move freely to help earn the family's living. Some historians argue that a wife and children provided free labor for a poor man; others note that some were too poor to marry at all. In short, the picture we have of the life of Hellenistic women varies according to their geographic and economic location. Wealthy, aristocratic women had more opportunities, and we have more information about their lives in the ancient sources than "ordinary" women, whose lives generally revolved around the domestic sphere of the patriarchal household.

Roman Women

The Roman matron lived a life very different from that of her lower-class contemporaries. Full participation in the Roman world depended not only on wealth but on citizenship, which granted the right to own and dispose of property. One could be born a citizen, earn or buy citizenship, or be granted it for favors rendered to Rome or a local Roman jurisdiction. Women who were married to citizens enjoyed relative economic and social securities that noncitizens did not have. (Even when the franchise became universal under Caracalla, it was only for men.) The Roman matron wore a long dress called a *stola* (as opposed to the togas worn by prostitutes) and a headband that publicly proclaimed her status. Such elite Roman women were likely to be involved in the economic, social, political, and religious life of republican and imperial Rome.

Roman legal theory regarding women rested on *infirmitas sexus*, the weakness of the sex, and mandated that women be under the custody and/or control of males. The *pater familias* had absolute control over his daughters, his power surpassing even that of her husband. (Many women were married *sine manu*, without passing legally from their fathers' to their husbands' family.) Fathers arranged marriages for their daughters (first marriages took place between the ages of twelve and fifteen), but the consent of both parties was required for marriage. Marriage and motherhood were not only expected; they were viewed by the Romans as patriotic duties. At age twenty there was by Augustinian legislation a penalty for unmarried women, and under the same legislation childlessness reduced the amount a woman could inherit. Tombstones show that mortality for women increased between fifteen and twenty-nine; the median age for the death of wives was thirty-four. The central person in a Roman marriage was the husband. A new wife was literally carried by him into his home and initiated into the cult of his family's hearth. The wife's task was to bear a son to perpetuate the male family line and allow clear transfer of the family's wealth and to be subject to her husband.

Still, many scholars think that the Roman Republic carried on and completed the Hellenistic move toward legal equality in marriage. Divorce was relatively easy to obtain in Rome, and either party could initiate the proceedings. No reason was legally required, but sterility was a frequent cause. According to the law of Augustus, adultery was a public offense only in women, not because of a breach in mutual fidelity but because of the threat it posed to a clear blood line of succession for a citizen's property. The children of a divorced couple remained with their father. Both widows and divorcees were encouraged to remarry, although the *univira*, a woman married only once, is frequently praised in inscriptions and texts of the period. In the Empire a woman was required to wait twelve months for remarriage to be sure she was not pregnant by her first husband. Augustus, who cared more about propagation, legislated that a widow between twenty and fifty could marry within the year. Women could inherit property from both fathers and husbands, and by the late Republic some women controlled large estates.

Contemporary descriptions of the ideal wife depict a woman who cares for her children, oversees the work of her slaves, and is skilled in spinning and weaving. The married Roman matron was responsible for the management of her house, which primarily involved supervising the slaves who did the work. Freed from domestic work, such women could make visits, shop, attend festivals and supervise the education of their children. Both male and female children of the wealthy had private tutors, though the girls usually did not study philosophy or rhetoric outside their homes and were usually married while boys were continuing their educations. It was believed that for the good of children both parents should be as educated as possible. There is ample evidence for many literate and intellectually competent women.

Since aristocratic Roman women were not sequestered, they did participate to some degree in public life. The patriotism of women during the Second Punic War has been noted and the first "women's demonstration" of which we have record in the West occurred in 195 B.C. when women gathered to demand the repeal of the Oppian Law, which limited their displays of status. Following the precedent set by the Hellenistic queens, the wives and consorts of Roman officials exerted considerable influence on politics. Antony's first wife, Fulvia, was especially influential, as was Octavia, the sister of Octavian, and the notorious Cleopatra of Egypt.

Coinage commemorated Roman women like Cornelia, usually for their production of children. There are numerous texts and inscriptions which praise Roman women, although scholars have noted that this is one way men exerted their own status. As Sarah Pomeroy (whose work I have used extensively here) has noted, the usual purpose of honoring women was to exalt their sons or husbands.

The lives of noncitizen, poor women and slaves were very different indeed. Amy Wordelman has pointed out that the Roman class structure resembled a pyramid, whose base was made up of slaves, former slaves, urban workers, and rural farmers and laborers. There was a small middle class of merchants, civil servants, and tradespeople, and the smallest category was the wealthy aristocrats at the top. (We have more evidence about their lives for obvious reasons.)

Slave women were legally classified as "property." They became slaves by birth to a slave mother, by capture in war, by kidnapping, and by being rescued from exposure at birth. (Female infanticide by exposure is widely attested as a common practice in all levels of Roman society.) The Roman economic system depended on labor provided by slaves. Although the work done by female slaves was more limited than that done by males, inscriptions on slave tombstones identify such women by the work they did: weaver, seamstress, midwife, nurse, servant, laundress, hairdresser, secretary, stenographer. It is noteworthy that several of these occupations required either apprenticeship or formal education or both. Roman households must have educated at least some of their slaves as well as their own children. And, of course, numbers of female slaves enhanced their owners' entourage.

Female slaves were sexually available to their masters and to his male slaves with his permission. Female slaves could also be sent out to work as prostitutes. Children born to a slave woman were her owner's property. Males were more highly valued, and female children were subject to exposure. Slaves could not enter into legal marriage, but could "cohabit," although their children were considered illegitimate. Slaves could, however, amass personal savings and buy their own slaves; so, for example, a male slave could buy his wife. According to the Lex Aelia Sentia of 4 A.D , the minimum age for manumission of slaves was thirty (the same as the average life expectancy for a woman), but slaves could be manumitted earlier and could buy their own freedom.

As was the case with Jewish women (who did, after all, live in the Roman world), it is probable that the majority of women at the time lived in rural areas. These women were slaves of citizen masters or lower-class free or citizen women. The latter worked as saleswomen of goods they or their families had grown or produced (for example, salt, fish, vegetables, spices, honey, cloth) or on small farms. They, like their upper-class sisters, also worked in wool. Urban poor women worked as waitresses (and as prostitutes), at laundries, in mills, and as butchers and fishmongers. (Some men's guilds apparently had female patronesses.) Very poor free women were probably worse off than slaves. On the positive side, affection was the principle reason for marriage among the lower classes, and tombstones indicate similar values to those of the upper classes: women were praised for family responsibility, industry, and for being married only once.

RELIGIOUS OPTIONS FOR GRECO-ROMAN WOMEN

There were three primary venues for the practice of Greco-Roman religions. Public religion was observed in the forum and in temples; semi-private cults were practiced in neighborhoods and citizen gatherings; and the family practiced its own religion in the household. In both the public and domestic cults, men wielded the primary sacerdotal responsibilities as magistrates, priests, *paterfamilias*. Perhaps the primary focus of religious life was domestic and conducted by the *paterfamilias* who performed the rites on behalf of those who were legally under his power, his wife (if they had been married *cum manu* releasing the woman from the power of her father and placing her under her husband's legal control), children, and slaves.

In the public sphere, there were two basic categories of religion, the native cults that supported the status quo and were, consequently, supported by the state, and oriental cults that were "imported" and a primary result of cultural cross-fertilization in the vast empire. The official Roman festivals were the mainstay of religious life and attended by the *matronae*. They included the Matronalia (March 1), when matrons offered flowers to Juno on the anniversary of the dedication of her temple; the Veneralia (April 1), celebrating Venus Verticordia and Fortuna Virilis (celebrated at the men's baths and organized around rites preceding the consummation of marriage); Bona Dea, honoring the goddess of women with a sacrifice at her temple on May 1 and with another gathering in early December at the home of the highest Roman magistrate; the Matralia (June 11), celebrated at the temple of the Mater Matuta in the cattle market as a fertility ritual; Fortuna Muliebris (July 6), commemorating the women who marched to the fourth milestone of the Via Latina and persuaded Coriolanus to lift his siege on Rome; and Nonae Caprotinae (July 7), which celebrated fertility in women by an offering of the sap of a wild fig tree to Juno. Other goddess cults marked significant transitions in women's lives. For example, girls from noble families dedicated their childhood togas to Fortuna Virginalis when they began to wear the *stola*.

Almost all we know of these cults comes from male writers, particularly Livy, Ovid, and Juvenal. This poses an interpretive dilemma, since such writers tended to impute sexual motives to women. It is hard to discern whether their reports are descriptive of what actually occurred, prescriptive in the sense of describing ideal situations they hoped for and supported, or condemnatory of behavior they considered "beyond the pale," out of male control. It is reasonably certain that women's religious roles were a corollary of their social station. Citizen women, especially those who could financially support festivals, might well serve as festival priestesses. A husband's religious or political preeminence was likely to lead to a more prominent cult role for his wife, although as both Bernadette Brooten and Ross Kraemer have shown, women held religious titles and served religious functions in their own right.

Of particular interest are the Vestal Virgins, six public priestesses whose function it was to tend the fire in the public hearth at the temple of Vesta in the Roman forum. That fire represented the father's power to give and sustain life, so they were, in effect, protectresses of the Roman male procreative power. The Vestals were chosen from noble families. They were to be between the ages of six and ten, have two living parents neither slaves nor in low-status occupations, be free from bodily defect, and under the authority of their fathers. The Vestals were taken by the *pontifex maximus* in a ceremony that resembled the Roman marriage ritual. They were to remain virginal for the thirty years of their service, after which they could marry (though few seem to have done so). The Vestals were severely regulated and could be put to death for infractions of chastity, but they were also among the most liberated of Roman women, since they were bound to neither father nor husband in a legal relationship. They were the only women in Rome permitted to drive in a two-wheeled wagon; they were preceded in the streets by a lictor; they had seats on the imperial podium and had legal privileges of men. They could testify in court, dispose of their own property, and make wills. The Vestals had a hand in every public sacrifice and were indirectly responsible for the fertility of Roman men. Their powerful position is interesting and ambiguous. They were virgins, wore the *stola* of matrons, and had the legal rights of men.

Amy Wordelman reminds us that in addition to participation in the state religious festivals, women belonged to a variety of private religious organizations. These groups usually had initiatory rites and moral and ritual obligations. They were formed around certain social classes or occupations and provided an arena in which women could exercise leadership functions. Prime among them were Jewish synagogues and Christian house-churches.

Close analysis of the native Roman religious cults indicates that their fundamental mythology supported the traditional roles for women of wives and mothers under the legal authority of fathers and husbands. This may be one reason why the "foreign," oriental religious cults were especially popular with women; such cults were uninterested in perpetuating Roman social order. The cult of Isis was particularly attractive to women and met with official resistance from the Romans (five times in the late Republic Isis shrines were ordered to be torn down), but retained considerable influence (and many scholars view it as a primary contender with Christianity for dominance in the Empire).

Isis was originally an Egyptian deity from about 2500 B.C. She had the attributes traditionally assigned to the male sky god: dominion over storms and wind, creator, giver of language, and healer. She was a single supreme goddess with many manifestations, and she promised her followers resurrection after death. The central myth of her cult involved her love for her son/husband, Osiris (they were lovers even in their mother's womb). Osiris was buried in a trunk in the Nile. In spite of discovering his marital infidelity, Isis raises Anubis, his child by another woman, searches for and finds his coffin, has sex with the body of her dead husband and thereby conceives his child, Horus. Osiris is subsequently dismembered by Typhon (husband of the women with whom he fathered Anubis), but Isis recovers the pieces of his body (save his penis) so that Osiris can return from the underworld to train Horus who avenges his father against Typhon.

In its Greco-Roman form the Isis cult emphasized death, mourning, and resurrection. Reenactments of Isis's mourning and joy were popular performances in the Greco-Roman world. Eroticism and asceticism mingled in her cult, which had no stake in either male dominance or class stratification. Isis mastered the universe, including fate, and so she provided protection in an uncertain world. (She was, for example, a patroness of sailors, and one of her great cult festivals involved the launching of a ship.) Interestingly, while Isis sanctioned authority and autonomy for women, her cult also stressed their traditional place in Roman society. Isis is first of all a wife who loves her husband and puts up with his infidelities, going so far as to raise his children by other women. (Since adultery was a crime only for Roman women and female slaves were sexually available to their masters in the household, one wonders how many Roman matrons found themselves in emotional circumstances not unlike Isis's.) As Ross Kraemer pointed out, the religion of Isis was the most favorable to women of any Roman cult. But while the Isis cult glorified a woman and showed her as equal or superior to her male consort, the adoration of a female deity did not necessarily improve the circumstances of the women who worshiped her nor raise the status of mortal women among men who followed the Isis cult. In fact, one of her strongest rival religions was the cult of Mithras, a masculine warrior god popular with the Roman army, whose worship was confined to males only.

This brief sketch of Roman state religions and the example of the oriental cult of Isis does not exhaust the religious possibilities for women. There were many other religious options as well as magic and divination, which were widely practiced at the time, and women as well as men participated. [For fuller discussions of this fascinating and complex topic see Franz Cumont, *The Oriental Religions in Roman Paganism* (New York: Dover, 1956); C. Kerenyi, *The Religion of the Greeks and Romans* (London: Thames & Hudson, 1962); Luther Martin, *Hellenistic Religions: An Introduction* (Oxford: Oxford University Press, 1987); Martin Nilson, *Greek Folk Religion* (New York: Harper & Row, 1961); and H. J. Rose, *Religion in Greece and Rome* (New York: Harper & Brothers, 1959).]

To summarize, a wide range of religious options was available to women in the Greco-Roman world. We do well to remember that Judaism and Christianity were but two among the many. Women clearly held offices in the religions of the ancient world, although the extent and power of those offices are difficult to determine because our sources of information about them are frequently biased. Inscriptional evidence indicates that women maintained temples and organized and financially supported festivals. While the priests of most Roman cults were men, the Sibylline oracles and the Vestal Virgins held famous and powerful office in public religion. While they frequently depended on family connections, women held cultic offices, especially when males were in short supply or unwilling to assume the financial cost of such public service. It is against this various and complex background that we must read the New Testament and what it says to and about women.

BIBLIOGRAPHY

Balsdon, J. P. V. D. *Roman Women, Their History and Habits.* London: The Bodley Head, 1962.

Brooten, Bernadette. *Women Leaders in the Ancient Synagogue.* Chico, Calif.: Scholars Press, 1982.

deCoulanges, N. D. F. *The Ancient City: A Study of the Religions, Laws and Institutions of Greece and Rome.* New York: Doubleday, 1955.

Goodwater, Leanna. *Women in Antiquity: An Annotated Bibliography.* Metuchen, N.J.: Scarecrow Press, 1975.

Jeremias, Joachim. *Jerusalem at the Time of Jesus.* Philadelphia: Fortress, 1969.

Kee, H. C. "The Changing Role of Women in the Early Christian World." *Theology Today* 49/2 (1992): 225–38.

Kraemer, Ross S. *Her Share of the Blessings: Women's Religions Among Pagans, Jews, and Christians in the Greco-Roman World.* New York: Oxford University Press, 1992.

_____, ed. *Maenads, Martyrs, Matrons, Monastics: A Sourcebook on Women's Religions in the Greco-Roman World.* Philadelphia: Fortress, 1988.

Lacey, W. K. *The Family in Classical Greece.* Ithaca, N.Y.: Cornell University Press, 1968.

Lefkowitz, Mary R., and Maureen B. Fant. *Women's Life in Greece and Rome.* Baltimore: Johns Hopkins University Press, 1982.

Loewe, Raphael. *The Position of Women in Judaism.* London: SPCK, 1966.

MacHaffie, Barbara J. *Her Story: Women in Christian Tradition.* Philadelphia: Fortress, 1986.

McClees, Helen. *A Study of Women in Attic Inscriptions.* New York: Columbia University Press, 1920.

Moore, G. F. *Judaism in the First Centuries of The Christian Era.* 3 volumes. Cambridge, Mass.: Harvard University Press, 1927–30.

Myers, Carol L. *Discovering Eve: Ancient Israelite Women in Context.* New York: Oxford University Press, 1988.

Neusner, Jacob. *A History of the Mishnaic Law of Women.* 5 volumes Leiden: Brill, 1980.

Otwell, John. *And Sarah Laughed: The Status of Women in the Old Testament.* Philadelphia: Westminster, 1977.

Pantel, Pauline S. *A History of Women in the West, Volume 1, From Ancient Goddesses to Christian Saints.* Cambridge, Mass.: Harvard University Press, 1992.

Pomeroy, Sarah B. *Goddesses, Whores, Wives, and Slaves: Women in Classical Antiquity.* New York: Schocken Books, 1975.

Ruether, Rosemary, and Eleanor McLaughlin, eds. *Women of Spirit: Female Leadership in the Jewish and Christian Traditions.* New York: Simon & Schuster, 1979.

Schaps, David M. *Economic Rights of Women in Ancient Greece.* Edinburgh: University Library, 1979.

Swidler, Leonard. *Women in Judaism: The Status of Women in Formative Judaism.* Metuchen, N.J.: Scarecrow Press, 1976.

Veyne, Paul, ed. *A History of Private Life: From Pagan Rome to Byzantium.* Cambridge, Mass.: Harvard University Press, 1987.

Wordelman, Amy L. "Everyday Life: Women in the Period of the New Testament." In *The Women's Bible Commentary,* edited by Carol A. Newsom and Sharon H. Ringe. Louisville: Westminster/John Knox, 1992.

3

The Pauline Letters

INTRODUCTION

PAUL HAS OFTEN BEEN VIEWED BY FEMINISTS as at best unsympathetic to women and, more probably, actively misogynistic. In George Bernard Shaw's turn of phrase, Paul has been viewed as "the eternal enemy of woman." In reading a great deal of secondary literature on the issue, I have come to think that this conclusion is sometimes reached on the basis of superficial readings of the Pauline corpus. Accurate interpretation of the writings of Paul on any subject is one of the most difficult tasks of New Testament scholarship, and the task is complicated by the frequently heated rhetoric that accompanies explorations of women's issues. I hope the following discussion will at least "coolly illuminate," if not make an original contribution to the discussion.

On the other hand, there are defenders of Paul's positive view of women. Among them is Robin Scroggs, whose 1972 article "Paul and the Eschatological Woman" set off a flurry of scholarly work on Paul's view of women in the church, activity that continues to the present moment. Scroggs held that Paul was the "only certain and consistent spokesman for the liberation and equality of women in the New Testament." Some agree. Many disagree. Before we enter the fray it is clarifying to survey Paul's life, situate his work in New Testament literature, and discuss various approaches that have been taken to his writings in the attempt to discover his position vis-à-vis women.

Who was this Paul who so influenced the development of early

Christianity? It is not as simple to write his biography from New Testament sources as it might appear. While the second half of the Acts of the Apostles apparently traces the career of Saul of Tarsus from his conversion to his final Roman imprisonment, many scholars believe that the work's author, Luke, was more a theologian than a historian. In short, there are serious problems with uncritical use of Acts as a source for the life of Paul, not the least of which is that it frequently disagrees with what Paul says about himself in various places in his letters. This can be seen clearly if one compares, for example, Acts 9 and 13–15 with Gal. 1:11–2:21. (A helpful summary of this issue and of Paul's life is found in D. Duling and N. Perrin, *The New Testament* [New York: Harcourt, Brace, 1994], chapter 6, "Paul, Apostle to the Gentiles.")

Keeping in mind these difficulties, a scenario of Paul's life might look something like the following: Paul was born close to the time of Jesus' birth in Hellenized Tarsus of a Jewish family with Roman citizenship. He may have been trained theologically under the Pharisee Gamaliel, but he was certainly a Pharisee and a persecutor of Christians before his dramatic conversion to Christianity when he was in his thirties. Thereafter followed a period of about fourteen years of retirement before he began active missionary journeys throughout the Mediterranean, Asia Minor, and Macedonia. The missionary period covered roughly ten years of travel and writing, 50 to 60 A.D., before he was imprisoned for his beliefs. In Philemon, one of his last authentic letters, Paul speaks of himself as "the aged" (*presbyteros*). Tradition originating with *1 Clement* (written in Rome during the 90s) assumes that Paul was martyred in Rome in the early 60s.

In his letters Paul makes reference to his strong Jewish background (Phil. 3:4–6), to his ability to make his own living by means of a trade (1 Cor. 4:12), and to a debilitating physical affliction (Galatians; 2 Cor. 12:7). He comes across both as a stern and commanding teacher and as a pastoral man with a particular genius for friendship. While Paul the man is as personally perplexing as he is spiritually astute, his overwhelming theological conviction is absolutely clear: Jesus of Nazareth is the long-awaited Messiah, and by means of him, God is extending the historical promises made to the Jews to all people. Paul understands his own call in terms of a mission to proclaim Jesus to the Gentile world. So Paul must always be understood as a man of three worlds and consequently three interconnected worldviews: Jewish, Greco-Roman, and Christian.

The letters that claim to come from the apostle Paul are the earliest writings in the New Testament. The dating of Paul's letters and exactly how many letters he himself wrote are vexing questions in New Testament scholarship. Careful reading suggests there were more letters than now survive (see 1 Cor. 5:9; 2 Cor. 2:4; and Col. 4:16). Some of the epistles we do have may be collections of several letters (2 Corinthians and Philippians, for example). Some letters traditionally attributed to Paul were probably written by his disciples. The Pastoral epistles (1 and 2 Timothy and Titus) and sometimes Colossians and Ephesians are taken to have been written after Paul died, "Deutero-Pauline." Scholarship generally concurs that most of the authentically Pauline letters were written in the 50s, and that works dated after 70 A.D. are probably pseudonymous. While there is little consensus about dating, the general order of the genuinely Pauline writings is taken by many scholars to be 1 Thessalonians, the Corinthian correspondence, Philippians, Galatians, Romans, Philemon, and possibly Colossians and Ephesians.

The point of all this for us is that the earliest records we have of the "Jesus movement" and of the church come from the pen of the apostle Paul. All of the scholarly, critical problems that one encounters in Pauline studies affect what we can learn of Paul's view on women, and they also present us with several specific problems. First, it must be borne in mind that Paul wrote for pastoral, not historical, reasons. That is, he wrote to the various churches to address issues of contemporary concern, not to document the development of early Christianity. What he says about women in the church is likely to be prescriptive rather than descriptive. That is, he may well be telling women in a particular church community what *to* do, not describing what they *are* doing. Second, whatever conclusion we come to about Paul as "pro" or "anti" woman, it is certainly true that he wrote from what Elisabeth Schüssler Fiorenza calls an "androcentric model." Paul used grammatically masculine language as if it were inclusive and understood men as normative and women as "special cases." Third, and for me crucially important, in his letters Paul is a thinker "in process." On more than one theological issue we see him working out his ideas, changing his views, which is another way to say that because Paul's writings are occasional they are not systematic and therefore not necessarily consistent. The various statements about women gleaned from Pauline sources *are* inconsistent!

Some of this inconsistency has to do with uncertain interpretation and the fact that some persons writing on Paul and women have ignored the composition history of the epistles, and some of it has to do with use of the sources. For example, six strongly anti-equality passages are often pointed to in the Pauline corpus: 1 Cor. 11:3–16, 14:34–35; Col. 3:18–19; Eph. 5:22–33; 1 Tim. 2:8–15; and Titus 2:4–5. But if we exclude Deutero-Pauline materials, only two occur in genuinely Pauline writings, and of those two, one (1 Cor. 14:34–35) is probably an interpolation (a later addition) and the other (1 Cor. 11:2–16) may well be. Thus, in determining what Paul thinks about women, it is important that, so far as we are able, we look at what *Paul* actually said to the degree that we can determine this. Moreover, many of the Pauline letters are also "from" others in addition to Paul: Silvanus and Timothy (1 Thessalonians), Sosthenes (1 Corinthians), Timothy (2 Corinthians; Philippians). There is no absolutely foolproof way to determine whether or not these associates "wrote" parts of the letters bearing their names along with Paul's. Certainly Deutero-Pauline works should be excluded or examined separately as I do here. In this study Colossians, Ephesians, and the Pastoral epistles have been set aside as post-Pauline and will be treated as a later development of the church's thinking about women. Within the apparently authentically Pauline corpus textual criticism must be consulted to determine if any of the passages dealing with women might be interpolations, later additions to the text. In 1 Corinthians, for example, 14:34–35 is widely thought to be a post-Pauline gloss and should not be included in Paul's arguments. When the authentic Pauline text has been determined, several hermeneutical principles should be applied. First, all texts should be read in their contexts. Second, it is important to struggle with the issue of which texts are normative and which are culturally conditioned. Third, passages which deal systematically with an issue should be used to clarify incidental references on the same subject found elsewhere.

Paul's writings as sources for information about the place of women in the early church, then, can be employed in a number of ways. One may look for texts which bespeak "principles," or may examine the prescriptive passages to see what instructions Paul actually gives to women. Or the epistles may be read to see what information can be gleaned about women in the church in a particular location. What, if anything, does Paul say descriptively about women in the churches?

Finally, one can seek to reconstruct from information available in passing references to women Paul knew and/or greeted a fuller picture of their roles in the churches.

In the discussion that follows, I have attempted to give an example of each kind of approach and to show what sort of information it might provide. Galatians 3:28 is presented as Paul's "principle" with regard to women in the church. I examine Paul's prescriptions with regard to women in 1 Corinthians, especially chapters 7 and 11. Using the material in Philippians and related sources, I briefly reconstruct a picture of the place of women in a Pauline church. And using the greetings in Romans 16 as source material, I present a view of the various roles women assumed in the Pauline churches. After presentation of the "principle," these discussions are arranged roughly chronologically in the order the letters were written to trace what appears to be Paul's developing thought on the matter and to assist in drawing conclusions about it.

Before turning to the readings of these passages, we do well to note that women existed as Christians and had leadership roles in the church *before* Paul began his evangelization. Although written after the Pauline letters, the Gospels depict women and their activities in the earliest Jesus movement. (See chapters 4 and 5 of this study.) And there were women who were already Christians in churches Paul visited. Priscilla and her husband, Aquila, were prominent Christians before Paul came to Corinth (1 Cor. 16:19; Rom. 16:5), as were Junia and her husband, Andronicus, before Paul visited Rome (Rom. 16:7). In Romans 16 Paul greets Phoebe, Prisca, Mary, Tryphaena, Tryphosa, Junia, Julia, and other women. In his letters Paul mentions these and other women as co-workers with no sense that they are subordinate to him. On the basis of Tryphaena and Tryphosa in Rome and Euodia and Syntyche in Philippi (and Mary and Martha of Bethany), Mary Rose D'Angelo argues that pairs of female workers characterized early Christianity's leadership. Certainly house-churches were the strongholds of Christianity in the New Testament period, and many of them were apparently led by women. Paul referred to the church in Corinth as "Chloe's people" (1 Cor. 1:11), and there were apparently at least three strong women in the Corinthian church, Chloe, Prisca, and Phoebe. Paul greets "Apphia our sister and Archippus our fellow soldier and the church in your house" (Philem. 2). Phoebe, who is mentioned in Rom. 16:1–2, was a deacon and patroness of the church at Cenchreae before Paul arrived on the scene. The glimpses we have of pre-Pauline Christianity in the Greco-Roman world suggest something of its egalitarian character. Women were prominent in the churches before Paul became a well-known apostle and evangelist. We might do well to read Paul against this "liberated" ecclesial background, for it may be that he is reacting to it and to all that it implied for the church in the empire.

BIBLIOGRAPHY

D'Angelo, M. "Women Partners in the New Testament." *JFSR* 6 (1990): 65–86.

Ellis, E. "Paul and His Co-Workers." *NTS* 17 (1971): 437–53.

Graham, R. "Women in the Pauline Churches: A Review Article." *Lexington Theological Quarterly* 11 (1976): 25–34.

Osborne, G. "Hermeneutics and Women in the Church." *JETS* 20 (1977): 337–52.

Schüssler Fiorenza, E., "Women in the Pre-Pauline and Pauline Churches." *Union Seminary Quarterly Review* 33 (1978): 153–66.

Scroggs, R. "Paul and the Eschatological Woman." *JAAR* 40 (1972): 283–303.

A PRINCIPLE: GALATIANS 3:28

The letter to the Galatians is attended by several scholarly questions, chief among them are the geographical destination of the letter and the identity of Paul's opponents there. In New Testament times "Galatia" signified both a territory in north central Asia Minor dominated by the Gauls and the Roman province that included the traditional Galatian territory plus portions of other ethnic areas. Scholars who think the letter was addressed to the north central territory hold what is called the Northern Galatian Hypothesis, while those who think the province proper is addressed hold the Southern Galatian Hypothesis. It is clear that Paul established the church in Galatia (1:8, 9 and 4:11ff. and apparently had a bout of illness in the process 4:13ff.) and then revisited it. The genuineness of the letter has never been questioned; it has always been considered to have been written by Paul and to be one of the best sources of information on his life. But there is lively discussion about the identity of the opponents whom Paul confronts.

The letter is addressed to Gentile Christians (1:9; 4:13) on whom Paul had imposed no Jewish requirements. It begins with Paul's surprise that they have turned so quickly from the gospel he preached (1:6) to one that would impose upon them the full requirements of the law (chapters 3–5). Paul writes about three years after his last visit to the church to defend his apostleship, authority, and gospel, as well as to arrest the progress of this "Judaizing" propaganda. There are three traditional points of view about Paul's opponents in Galatia. Some scholars think they were Jewish-Christian syncretists who advocated circumcision for its symbolic character. Some believe they were Gentiles who had themselves recently become converts of a Judaizing Christian movement in Galatia. And some believe they were "men from James" (2:11), agitators moved by political nationalism to assert the requirements of Torah. Whoever precisely they were, they stressed the demands of the law and circumcision as binding upon all Christians, whether their origins were Jewish or Gentile. Paul vigorously opposes this view, arguing that the cross of Christ is the true instrument of salvation which is a free gift from God.

The letter is crucial in early Christianity as one of the first statements of Gentile Christian theology and self-definition. It establishes that Gentiles need not be circumcised to be full members of the Christian community, that table fellowship is possible between Jewish and Gentile Christians, and that Christianity is, in fact, a universal religion in its own right apart from its Jewish origins. It is particularly noteworthy for the autobiographical statements about Paul in chapters 1 and 2, and for our study of women in the New Testament because it provides what most scholars think to be Paul's primary theological statement on women's position in the church, Gal. 3:28: "There is no longer Jew or Greek, there is no longer slave or free, there is no longer male and female; for all of you are one in Christ Jesus."

This remarkable statement, which is taken by many scholars to be part of an early Christian baptismal liturgy, effectively sets aside the ethnic, economic, and gender boundaries of the Greco-Roman world. It occurs at the end of Paul's discussion of Abraham, whom Paul uses as an example to refute the need for circumcision because God had declared Abraham righteous *before* he was circumcised. Abraham "believed God, and it was reckoned to him as righteousness" (3:6). The point is that it is faith in God and not the requirements of the law that make one righteous. In Christ Jesus all are "children of God by faith"

(3:24). In a letter on which there is little scholarly agreement, most scholars nevertheless concur that Gal. 3:28 is as close as we come to having a statement of Paul's theological conviction vis-à-vis women in the church.

In the context of Diaspora Judaism Paul argues that baptism destroys the boundaries society erects between people (3:27). Value judgments based on ethnic origin (Jew/Greek), economic status (slave/free), or gender (male/female) should no longer hold in the Christian community. More than one scholar has noted that Gal. 3:28 is not uniquely Pauline in thought. Origins of the idea have been traced both to dominical sayings in the *Gospel of the Egyptians*, where "neither male nor female" referred to social unification, and to a variety of sources in rabbinic Judaism, where these sets of three pairs function as merisms (statements in which a whole is represented by mentioning pairs of extremes). Especially the rabbinic parallels to Gal. 3:28 contrast persons of high and low status; by their use here Paul insists that both can be brought together in the church (and compare 1 Cor. 12:13 and Col. 3:10–11).

The equality and unity of men and women in the church, their "oneness in Christ Jesus," is especially important in light of the larger issue in Galatians. If the church were to insist on circumcision as a requirement for full church membership, then women would be automatically excluded from full status in the community. Paul rejects an initiatory rite that systematically favors one group (males) and excludes another (female). This is particularly striking in a world in which male superiority over females was a "given," especially in the religious sphere. Many scholars have noted the popularity of Christianity among women in the Empire, the theoretical basis for which may be found here. Gal. 3:28 argues for the ontological equality of the pairs mentioned after baptism into Christ, though not necessarily that each has the same function within the Christian community. This qualification is an important one, for it suggests the gap which, in fact, existed between the statement of principle set forth and both Paul's more practical injunctions and the practice of the churches.

While Gal. 3:28 is the one "principle" with special relevance to women, it should be noted that in this letter Paul makes special mention of the fact that God's son was "born of a woman" (4:4), refers to himself as the mother who is in the process of giving birth to the Galatian church (4:19), and uses the example of the matriarchs Sarah and

Hagar to show the superiority of faith over law (4:21–31). Finally, in suggesting that the Christians in Galatia should use their freedom to become "slaves to one another" (5:13), Paul is lifting up the traditionally female values of service as appropriate to *all* members of the church, both men and women.

BIBLIOGRAPHY

Boucher, M. "Some Unexplored Parallels to 1 Cor 11:2–12 and Gal. 3:28: The New Testament on the Role of Women." *CBQ* 31 (1969): 50–58.

Osiek, C. "Galatians." In *The Women's Bible Commentary*, edited by C. Newsom and S. Ringe, 333–37. Louisville: Westminster/John Knox, 1992.

Witherington, B. "Rites and Rights for Women—Galatians 3:28." *NTS* 27 (1981): 593–604.

A PRESCRIPTIVE SOURCE: 1 CORINTHIANS

Corinth was a major city of antiquity which controlled the isthmus between mainland Greece and the Peloponnesus. Much of its wealth came from commerce between the Adriatic and Aegean seas. Ancient Corinth was destroyed by the Roman General Mummius in 146 B.C. and was reconstructed by Julius Caesar in 44 B.C. In Paul's time it was the largest and most modern city in Greece with a population of about four hundred thousand. Archibald Robertson and Alfred Plummer's classic commentary on Paul's letter to the Corinthians (*The First Epistle of St. Paul to the Corinthians* [New York: Charles Scribner's Sons, 1911]) called it "the Empire in miniature." Augustus made it the capital of the new Roman province of Achaea and that, along with its strategic location, may have been Paul's attraction to it as a missionary headquarters.

In his *Introduction to the New Testament* (Philadelphia: Fortress, 1982), Helmut Koester of Harvard concluded that Luke is more reliable in his reporting on Corinth than on any other Pauline city. According to Luke, Paul arrived in Corinth from Athens (probably in the early 50s). Christians already lived there when he arrived, probably persons driven from Rome by the Edict of Claudius (48/49 A.D.). Priscilla and

Aquila were Christians before Paul arrived; Paul stayed and worked with them during his tenure in the city. In spite of a suit brought against him before Gallio (in the fall of 51?), Paul stayed in Corinth roughly a year and a half. His associates there included Timothy and Silvanus (co-authors of 1 Thessalonians, which was written from Corinth), Stephanas, and Apollos (a Jewish-Christian from Alexandria who received further training from Priscilla and Aquila). Paul's earliest converts in the city were Stephanas and his household, Crispus, and Gaius, all men (1:14–15). Although there were some Jews among them, the majority of Corinthian Christians were Gentile and of the lower socioeconomic order (1:26). Jerome Murphy O'Connor reports that at Paul's time there were forty to fifty Christians in Corinth, of whom we know seventeen by name. Paul's expulsion from Corinth, which is reported in Acts 18:12–18, was probably edited by Luke to placate a Roman audience, but Paul was forced to leave Corinth by Gallio, probably in the spring of 52.

Paul's work in Corinth was characteristic of his missionary method. He settled in the capital of a province with a few trustworthy associates, usually including some women, gathered the Christians already in the area, and employed their services to found congregations nearby. Phoebe, deacon of the church in the nearby port city of Cenchreae, was probably one of these converts (see Rom. 16:1–2). During absences from the church he founded, Paul kept contact by means of letters. His was not the work of a "lone ranger," but an organized mission work which included the writing of epistles as part of the church's development.

The occasion of the writing of 1 Corinthians seems to have been an oral report on conditions in the church brought to Paul in Ephesus (16:8) by a delegation from "Chloe's people" (1:11) and a letter that the Corinthian church had written seeking his advice (7:1; 8:1; 12:1; 16:1). Paul talked with the members of the letter delegation to get more information about the situation of the church (16:17). He had already written to the church at least once (5:9). It is noteworthy that the delegation to Paul came from what must have been either a house-church in the home of a woman, Chloe, or a Christian community led by her. Nothing in the text suggests that Paul disapproved of this arrangement. It is so clearly accepted that Paul makes no mention of it other than to note that his information came from "Chloe's people" (1:11).

The text of 1 Corinthians is divided between matters Chloe's church reported to Paul (chapters 2–5) and matters the Corinthians had written Paul for advice about (chapters 6–15). The prescriptive materials directed specifically to women occur in the latter section and include 7:1–40; 11:3–16; and 14:34–36. Apparently the church itself was struggling with the place of women. Given the position of women in the Empire (see the previous chapter) and Paul's "principle" in Gal. 3:28, it is not difficult to understand how conflict might have arisen. Before examining these passages, then, a note on the general situation of women in Corinth is in order.

As was noted in the first chapter, the legal equality of women in the Greek cities was more limited than in the Roman, but was an improvement over the position of women in Palestine. Culturally, Corinth had been Roman since 44 B.C., so the position of women there was more analogous to that in Roman cities. Girls in such cities married between the ages of twelve and fourteen, men at around twenty. Burial records suggest that life expectancies of females were about seven years shorter than those of men, probably due to death in childbirth. Infanticide by exposure was widely practiced, and more girls babies were exposed than boys because of the financial burden the dowry system placed on the families of female children. Thus, in many Greco-Roman cities there were significantly fewer women than men, increasing the pressure on them to marry early and bear children. To do so was to be a "loyal citizen," to demur smacked of social disruption.

One of the general problems that Paul seems to have encountered in the church in Corinth was the existence of a group of pneumatics, or spiritual people, who, on the basis of their spiritual experiences set themselves apart from other members of the Christian community, and in their "pentecostal" behavior threatened order in the community. Several scholars have pointed out that women prophets may well have constituted a large percentage of this group. And those women prophets might well have preferred single, celibate lives for the freedom it offered them. Paul himself associated sexual abstinence with prayer (7:5), and the women prophets in Corinth were known for prayer (11:5).

In her extensive study of women in Corinth, *The Corinthian Women Prophets* (Philadelphia: Fortress, 1990), Antoinette Clark Wire has argued from careful analysis of Paul's rhetoric that those women's understanding of the gospel led them publicly to claim freedom and leadership in the community in such a way that Paul's authority was threatened. She thinks that this group of women prophets withdrew from sexual relations (7:1–40), claimed freedoms like eating meat offered to idols and removing their head coverings (11:2–16; 8:1–13; 10:1–33), and proclaimed God's wisdom in public meetings through ecstatic speech (chapters 12–14). Wire believes that, in theory, Paul granted the women the freedom they claimed in Christ, but that he was critical of how they were exercising it at the expense of the community.

While there have been serious scholarly questions raised about Wire's methodology, her work has pointed out that far from being ancillary to the issues in 1 Corinthians, the place of women in that church is central to Paul's concerns. Because it was standard practice in Greco-Roman polemic to attack philosophical and religious movements by attacking the behavior of their women, the public deportment of the Christian women in Corinth was an issue not only of church order but of the reputation of the church in the larger society. I think that issue is frequently at the forefront of Paul's discussion of beliefs and, subsequently, practices of the Corinthian church, and especially in his prescriptive remarks to and about women.

Chapter 7, the chapter on marriage and sexual relations, provides a particularly clear example of this assertion. Paul addresses an issue the Corinthians have raised ("Now concerning the matters about which you wrote") by quoting their position; "it is well for a man not to touch a woman" (7:1). The Corinthians have apparently put the case to Paul that it is better for Christians to live lives of sexual asceticism. They apparently expect Paul to agree with them. Note that the doubts about marriage in the chapter are theirs, not Paul's. Although Paul wishes that "all were as I myself am" (that is, single, v. 7 and compare vv. 39–40) because he believes that "the present form of this world is passing away" (v. 31), because he wants them to be "free from anxieties" (v. 32) attendant upon the married state, and because he is concerned about the possibility of sexual immorality (vv. 2, 5, 9, 36), he does not agree that Christians should renounce marriage and sexual relations within marriage. To do so would be an affront to commonly held views about marriage in Roman society and a danger to community morality.

Refraining from marriage and, subsequently, procreation was frowned upon in both Jewish and Roman society. Jews were expected to marry, and males who did not were suspect. After the Augustan marriage laws, those who refused to marry and procreate were penalized in various ways by the government. As we noted in chapter 2 of this study, for Romans the purpose of marriage was the production of male heirs to continue the name, property, and family religion of the husband. Marriage and stable families were associated with the stability of the state. With the exception of the Cynics, philosophical schools in the period supported marriage. If the Christian community not only practiced but taught abstinence from marriage, it would fly directly in the face of contemporary convention, and Paul knows this.

Many scholars and commentators have noted the remarkable equality with which Paul presents the issues in chapter 7. He speaks to both men and women in regard to conjugal relations (vv. 2–5), to divorce (vv. 10–11), to marriage to unbelievers (vv. 12–16) and to anxiety (vv. 32–34). In fact 1 Corinthians 7 presents the same pairs as Gal. 3:28—Greek/Jew or circumcised/uncircumcised (vv. 17–19), slave/free (vv. 21–23), and male/female. Paul speaks of women "separating" and men "divorcing," and then of women "divorcing" and men "separating" (7:13, 15), in effect, removing sex-linked legal distinctions. This mutuality is noteworthy, as is the fact that Paul does not mention the procreation of children when he writes of marriage (nor, note, of the joyful pleasure of sexual expression the couple shares), nor does he charge women with immorality anywhere in the letter. But "equality" is not Paul's focus here. The community's reputation is. (Notice, however, that there are more verses directed to women than to men and that when Paul instructs widows, he makes no reference to their male counterparts.)

While Paul, who still apparently expects an imminent parousia, might prefer celibacy for Christians in a world that is passing away, he knows that position both affronts Roman mores and runs the risk of leading to immorality within the Christian community because of Christians unable to live up to the ideal standard of celibacy. That, in turn, would diminish the church's reputation in the eyes of outsiders. (Recall that the Corinthian church is already suffering from moral lapses in the sexual arena; see 1 Corinthians 5.) Paul wants both to diminish the risks of sexual immorality within the community and to reduce the chance of criticism from without. In short, as Margaret MacDonald has pointed out, Paul was striving to curtail social disruption in Corinth. Thus, he counsels marriage—"by way of concession, not of command" (v. 6)—because he has "no command of the Lord" (v. 25), only his own opinion, which, of course, comes with apostolic authority, and "the spirit of God" (v. 40). Paul steers clear of absolutism in his instructions with regard to marriage. He maintains the practical advantages of celibacy, but for equally practical reasons refuses to command it. At the same time, Paul surprises us by allowing that unmarried women not only can, but should, if possible, remain unmarried (vv. 8, 39–40), a striking point of view in the cultural circumstances.

Increasing visibility of women prophets and female celibates in the church undoubtedly made it look more and more subversive to outsiders. That concern for "public opinion" is also at work in 1 Cor. 11:2–16, one of the most problematic passages in the Pauline corpus. It should be noted at the outset that a growing number of New Testament scholars believe that 11:2–15 is an interpolation in 1 Corinthians. Chapters 10 and 11 hold together as a consistent argument without vv. 2–16, and most of the material in 10:1–11:2 and 11:17–34 allude in some way to Israel's wilderness experience, imagery that is absent from 11:2–16. Verses 2 and 17 of chapter 11 are closely linked by repetitions of significant words and vv. 2–16 contain many words that occur nowhere else in the Pauline corpus or the New Testament. In fact, the closest parallel to 1 Cor. 11:2–16 is Eph. 5:21–24, which many scholars take to be Deutero-Pauline, and 1 Tim. 2:13–15, which almost certainly is. The genuine Pauline corpus, it is argued, contains no passages which advocate male supremacy and female subordination, and that fact, together with the textual evidence suggests that this passage is from a later generation of Christians who were concerned about the prominence of women in the community. (For fuller discussion of the issue, see G. W. Trompf, "On Attitudes Toward Women in Paul and Paulinist Literature: I Cor 11:3–16 and its Context," *CBQ* 42 [1980]: 196–215; and W. O. Walker, "I Corinthians 11:2–16 and Paul's Views Regarding Women," *JBL* 94 [1975]: 94–110.)

Although I personally find the textual arguments that 1 Corinthians 11:2–16 is an interpolation convincing, because the scholarly community has not reached consensus on the issue, I include a brief discussion of the passage here. Having noted that it breaks the flow of the argument in chapters 10 and 11, the next feature worthy of comment is that the passage, in fact, *assumes* that women pray and prophesy publicly in the Christian community. It is not the women's right and privilege to do so that is in question, but the manner of their exercise of this function. As the NRSV note in *The Oxford Annotated Bible* suggests, "propriety in dress at public prayer" is the issue.

Or is it? The passage is notoriously difficult both to translate and to interpret. Its logic is unclear and its reasoning tortuous. The usual reading of the passage is that the author understands head covering as a sign of subordination of women to men, which is appropriate since all women shared Eve's guilt. Furthermore, for a woman to show her head uncovered in public was compared to shaving it (v. 5) and thus disrespecting her own nature. But there are significant difficulties with such a reading. First, why appeal to the sin of Eve in a largely Gentile congregation on whom the logic might be lost? Second, there is no basis for assuming that a hellenized Jew would assume that *kephalē*, ("head") meant "having authority." Rather, as a number of recent studies have conclusively proved, it meant something more like "origin of" or "source." It is inappropriate to read twentieth-century connotations back into a first-century term.

Third, the word "veil" does not occur in the passage, nor does any Greek word for a headdress. And in any case, the common assumption that men did not wear veils in antiquity is mistaken. Head covering was part of the Roman way of worship and is even attested by a statue from the Augustan period in Corinth of a veiled man. In statuary veils are found on rulers and other men during worship (usually, it is thought, as a symbol of piety and conservative religion), and on religious functionaries, both male and female. In mourning, Roman men covered their heads. (For more information, see C. L. Thompson, "Hair styles, Head-coverings, and St. Paul: Portraits from Roman Corinth," *Biblical Archaeologist* 51 [1988]: 99–115.)

In vv. 5, 6, and 7 the word often translated into English by "veil" is some form of *kalyptō*, meaning "to cover." "Veil" is assumed by many translators, but the word is not there. Verse 10 is very interesting. It literally says that a woman ought to have *exousia* ("authority") over her head. Again, this is usually translated "veil" in English, but the Greek word clearly means "authority." On the basis of this fact Morna Hooker has argued that, rather than a sign of subordination, the "head covering" of the Corinthian women, whatever it was, is the symbol of their authority to do what they were doing. On their heads is the symbol of their authority to pray and prophesy in the community (M. Hooker, "Authority on the Head: An Examination of I Corinthians 11:10," *NTS* 10 [1963–64]: 410–16).

A somewhat similar argument is set forward by Jerome Murphy-O'Connor ("Sex and Logic in 1 Cor. 11:2–16," *CBQ* 42 [1980]: 482–500). He points out that, as was the case in chapter 7, the writer here (whom he assumes to be Paul) addresses both men and women equally; in v. 5 women perform the same functions as men in worship and are criticized in the same way. Since a veil is not mentioned and the passage moves toward direct instructions with regard to hair length (vv. 14–15), Murphy-O'Connor thinks the issue must be hairstyle or disordered hair, perhaps refusal to do the hair in a way proper to women at the time. Paul's argument proceeds along lines of argument from the order of creation (vv. 3, 7–12), the teaching of nature (vv. 13–15), and the custom of the churches (v. 16). Paul thought women had the authority to act as they were acting in the community's worship, but by means of their properly coiffed hair needed to convey their new status to the angels who watched for breaches of law. (These angels and their function are one of the knottiest problems in the passage.) Woman's new power and equality are related to her being fully woman, and her properly done hair is a symbol of both. Moreover, properly arranged hair would make such a woman acceptable in Jewish circles, where loose hair was a symbol of uncleanness (see Num. 4:18; Lev. 13:45) and would set her apart from ecstatic worshipers in Greco-Roman religions like, for example, those who let their hair down as part of their worship of Isis.

It seems unlikely that the puzzles presented by this passage will ever be completely solved. But without a clear reading of the whole passage it is still possible to glean some information about women in Corinth, and perhaps about Paul's view of their activity (although such conclusions are provisional). The author of the passage assumes, first, that both men and women pray and prophesy in the congregation (vv. 4–5) and that, second, the women who do so would consider themselves honorable. For the activity to be seemly, proper covering or uncovering of the head (with hair? with veils?) is important as a mark of social order within the community. It is unclear whether subordination of woman to man is the issue so much as order in the church assembly. (This certainly is an issue in the larger context of the passage, chapters 11–14, which address propriety in worship.) In fact, the author makes a clear statement of the interdependence of Christian men and women; "in the Lord woman is not independent of man or man independent of woman" (v. 11). The conclusion of the passage is noteworthy for its inconclusiveness; "if anyone is disposed to be contentious—we have no such custom, nor do the churches of God" (v. 16). If the passage is an appeal for equivalence in sexual roles, it concedes little, although it does make clear that the crucial functions of prayer and prophecy were carried out in the Christian community of Corinth by men and women without any distinctive sign of the subordinate status of women.

If 1 Cor. 11:2–16 is sometimes taken to be an interpolation in the letter and thereby proves to be a spurious source for Paul's views on the position of women in that church, 1 Cor. 14: 34–35 is almost universally taken to be an interpolation. In addition to the fact that these verses contradict Paul's views in the longer passage just examined, where it is assumed that women pray and prophesy publicly, they occur in different points in the argument in some of the early manuscripts of the New Testament. (In some manuscripts, for example, they occur at the very end of chapter 14.) In an article examining all the possible interpolations in the letter, Jerome Murphy-O'Connor concludes that only the arguments for 4:6 and 14:34–35 as interpolations are convincing (see "Interpolations in I Cor.," *CBQ* 48 [1986]: 81–94). How, then, did these verses get into the letter? Some scholars view them as quotations of the Corinthians' position, like those in 7:1; 8:1, 4–6. A more likely possibility is that vv. 34 and 35 were originally marginal glosses, comments on the text written in the margin by an early reader, which in later copying of the manuscript were incorporated into the text.

The argument could be made that although Paul presupposed the public participation of women in the church assemblies in chapter 11, growing concern over the disorderly conduct of public worship led him to withdraw from his earlier position. To my way of thinking, however, these verses agree not with Paul's own views as they are represented here in 1 Corinthians and in Galatians, but with those of later writers, like the author of 1 Tim. 2:11–12 and 1 Pet. 3:1–6. How were Christian women like Prisca (Rom. 16:3; 1 Cor. 16:19) and Phoebe (Rom. 16:1–2), of whom Paul obviously approved, to carry out their function if they could not speak publicly? It is illogical to think that Paul would commend women while he silences them. And in any case, the verses seem to apply only to married women, which is odd since Paul allows for and even commends unmarried women in the Christian assembly (chapter 7). The most logical conclusion about 1 Cor. 14:34–35 is that it does not come from the hand of the apostle Paul and therefore does not represent his opinion.

To summarize, then, 1 Corinthians is a particularly good example of how difficult it is to determine Paul's own prescriptions with regard to Christian women. Other issues are usually in focus, and women, when they are mentioned, are frequently mentioned in passing. In short, Paul has little to say directly to women. That said, nowhere in 1 Corinthians does the apostle specifically limit the activity of Christian women in the community or criticize women as women for the exercise of their charisms (gifts). I think this, in itself, is significant.

BIBLIOGRAPHY

Bassler, J. "I Corinthians." In *The Women's Bible Commentary*, edited by C. Newsom and S. Ringe, 321–29. Louisville: Westminster/ John Knox, 1992.

Caird, G. B. "Paul and Women's Liberty." *Bull. John Rylands Library* 54 (1972): 268–81.

MacDonald, M. Y. "Women Holy in Body and Spirit: The Social Setting of I Cor. 7." *NTS* 36 (1990): 161–81.

Murphy-O'Connor, Jerome. *St Paul's Corinth*. Wilmington, Del.: M. Glazier, 1983.

Schüssler Fiorenza, E. "Women in the Pre-Pauline and Pauline Churches." *Union Seminary Quarterly Review* 33 (1978): 153–66.

Ward, R. B. "Paul: How He Radically Re-defined Marriage." *Bible Review* 4 (1988): 26–31.

A RECONSTRUCTION: PHILIPPIANS

When one seeks to reconstruct the position of women in the Pauline church at Philippi, a wealth of material is available. In addition to the Philippian letter, there is the Lukan material in Acts 16 (which is treated more extensively in this study in chapter 5), the letter of Polycarp (bishop of Smyrna in the middle of the second century) to the Philippians, the apocryphal *Acts of Paul* (probably written in the latter half of the second century), the *Acts of Andrew*, and evidence of "pagan" religious practice as well as extensive archaeological material and inscriptions from the post-Constantinian church. This material has been carefully presented by Valerie Abrahamsen in her article "Women at Philippi: The Pagan and Christian Evidence," *JFSR* 3 (1987): 17–30, and I am indebted to her work in what follows, although for our purposes here, I shall confine my remarks primarily to evidence gleaned from the biblical books Acts and Philippians and the letter of Polycarp to the Philippians, which is just within the New Testament period, with only peripheral mention of the other sources.

According to Luke, while in Troas Paul had a vision of a Macedonian who summoned him for help (Acts 16:6–10; in v. 10 the "we" material in Acts commences). The apostle set sail and arrived in Philippi (probably about 50 A.D.), where he first preached on the Sabbath to women outside the city at a "place of prayer" and founded his first European congregation upon the foundation of a female convert, Lydia, and her household (16:11–15). Having freed a slave girl from an oracular spirit, Paul, Silas, and Timothy are imprisoned, but later freed by an earthquake with the subsequent conversion of their jailer and his household. After their trial and a visit with Lydia, the missionaries departed for Thessalonica (Acts 16:16–17:1).

The church founded at Philippi was always one of Paul's favorites. It apparently received one or two further visits from him (1 Cor. 16:5–6; 2 Cor. 2:13; 7:5), and we have one extant letter in the New Testament addressed to the church. While no scholar doubts its authenticity, there is lively debate about whether it is a literary unity or a "patchwork" consisting of as many as three fragments of prior letters: 4:10–20 written from prison before Epaphroditus's illness; 1:1–3:1; 4:4–7; and 2:21–23, a second letter; and 4:8–9 derived from a letter written when Paul was no longer in prison.

Whatever the literary history of the letter, the version we have indicates that Paul wrote it as a thank you for the contribution brought to him by Epaphroditus (2:25; 4:18), which he used as an occasion to appeal to the church to maintain its unity. The pervading tone is of strong personal attachment and affection, and the letter is almost entirely commendatory. Paul, who is imprisoned at the time of the writing (1:7, 13, 14, 17) at a place frequented by the praetorian guard and Caesar's household, has confidence in the Philippian church. Because his authority there has not been attacked or challenged, we see a different, "softer" Paul.

It is important to recall that this church, which was so favored by the apostle, was a church founded in an area known for the worship of goddesses and begun among women converts. It was a church in which women continued to play significant leadership roles. In antiquity, the cults of Diana and Isis were both popular in Philippi. The sanctuary of Diana was well known in the imperial period and apparently attracted both male and female worshipers. As noted in the previous chapter, Isis was also served by functionaries of both sexes and was one of the most popular deities in the Empire, probably because her cult spoke directly to human need in the realm of fertility, healing, and the afterlife. Because religious belief and practice at the time was fluid, it would have been difficult to convince Christians of the need for exclusive loyalty to Jesus Christ. The church, in short, probably had a real struggle with pagan religions with strong female deities.

Perhaps in part because women were already a force in religious life in Philippi, the Philippian church took root among them. The church first met in the home of Lydia (Acts 16:15, 40), and so it may well be that the letter (or letters) was directed there. Certainly Luke portrays Paul as having had no qualms about making his headquarters in her home. The letter itself mentions by name two women who continued to be leaders in the congregation, Euodia and Syntyche (4:2–3). The usual reading of this brief passage is that the two women have had a disagreement and need to be reconciled, and while that may be part of what is at work here, the language of v. 3 suggests something of their importance in the church. They have "labored side by side" (*synēthlē-san*) with Paul "in the gospel," and he calls them "fellow workers" (*synergōn*) with Clement and "the rest." As Paul uses the term "fellow workers" (or its cognate *ergatēs*) elsewhere, it refers to itinerant workers, those who traveled to spread the gospel. As E. Earl Ellis has noted, the term refers to a great many prominent early Christians, both men and women.

The meaning of *synēthlēsan* is less clear. The RSV translation stresses a similarity of ministry shared by Paul, Euodia, Syntyche, and Clement. Does that mean simply that they worked with Paul (say, in his tent making)? Or were they fellow preachers or presiders in the community's worship? The word is used at only one other place in the New Testament, Phil. 1:27, where Paul commands the entire Philippian church to strive together. The verb *synathleō* carries the sense of cooperation in the face of hostility and could be used of cooperation in war or in the games (both masculine metaphors that Paul uses illustratively in this letter). Whatever the precise meaning of the term, Euodia and Syntyche are apparently another example of a female missionary couple who devoted themselves to the work of the church and the spread of the gospel and of whom Paul knew and approved.

By the time Polycarp of Smyrna wrote to the Philippians (about the middle of the second century) the circumstances of the church had changed dramatically (see chapter 6 of this study). The letter is written both to commend the church and to exhort it to further growth, as well as to defend the Pauline gospel. Polycarp devotes most of chapter 4 of the letter to instructions about wives and women. His overall message is that women must behave in ways that do not bring the church into disrepute. He speaks of the training of wives, but does not think of them as servants of their husbands nor does he attempt to limit their lively interest in the faith. So long as a wife maintained marital fidelity to her husband, Polycarp allowed her social access to both men and women in the community (4:2). While he doesn't clearly describe their work, Polycarp notes that an order of widows existed in Philippi who were expected to live exemplary lives and to offer public prayers and private prayers "for all" (4:3). "Virgins" (*parthenous*) are exhorted to "walk with a blameless and pure conscience" (5:3), which suggests that, as in the church at Corinth, there were women living celibate lives in and for the church. At the end of the letter, Polycarp specifically commends Crescens's sister, who is coming to Philippi, apparently to be of service to the church (14:1).

Apocryphal writings from the late second century and beyond, the *Acts of Paul* and the *Acts of Andrew*, both mention Philippi in passing. In a fragment of the *Acts of Paul*, Longinus orders the death of his daughter, Frontina, and of Paul, who had converted her to a celibate form of Christianity. The girl is killed as non-Christian witnesses flee, only to be later converted when the girl is restored to life. Similarly in the *Acts of Andrew*, Exuos, a wealthy young Thessalonian, becomes a Christian and renounces his inheritance. This angers his parents enough to ignite the house where he is staying with Andrew, but the latter miraculously puts out the fire with holy water. While these apocryphal stories are legendary, they do suggest that an ascetic form of Christianity was practiced in and around Philippi in the generation or so after Paul.

Finally, a fourth-century basilica excavated in Philippi revealed inscriptions from the fourth to sixth centuries that list women as deacons and canonesses. References to female deacons suggests that one, Agatha, was buried with her husband, John; and the other, Posidonia, was buried with a woman named Pancharia, a canoness (another set of female partner church workers?). While the word "deacon" is used in the New Testament for the first time in Phil. 1:1 and suggests functions that were similarly carried out by men and women, the term "canoness" has been ascribed only to women at Philippi and suggests an order of consecrated virgins or widows, perhaps like those described in 1 Timothy and alluded to by Polycarp.

In summary, the picture we have of the church in Philippi in the first centuries of our era is remarkably consistent; it is that of a community with prominent women leaders. Luke reports that women were the first converts in the area, and Paul's letter (letters?) to the church (which may have been directed to Lydia's house-church) commends Euodia and Syntyche, who had worked with him in the area. Women continue to attract the attention of later bishops writing to the church and appear in legendary material, suggesting that they continued to be important both historically and in the popular imagination. There is no hint in the New Testament material on Philippi, and certainly none in Paul's letter, of limitation on women who were prominent in the church. In fact, in the words of W. D. Thomas, at Philippi we glimpse something of the new status that the church afforded to women, especially, I would add, in an area where women historically were prominent in the local religious cults.

BIBLIOGRAPHY

D'Angelo, M. R. "Women Partners in the New Testament." *JFSR* 6 (1990): 65–86.

Ellis, E. E. "Paul and His Co-Workers." *NTS* 17 (1971): 437–53.

Gillman, F. M. "Early Christian Women at Philippi." *Journal of Gender in World Religions* 1 (1990): 59–79.

Malinowski, F. X. "The Brave Women of Philippi." *Biblical Theology Bulletin* 15 (1985): 60–64.

Portefaix, L. *Sisters Rejoice: Paul's Letter to the Philippians and Luke-Acts as Received by First Century Philippian Women*. Uppsala: Almqvist & Wiksell, 1988.

Thomas, W. D. "Lydia: A Truly Liberated Women." *ExpTms* 95 (1984): 112–13.

———. "The Place of Women in the Church at Philippi." *ExpTms* 83 (1972): 117–20.

THE GREETINGS: ROMANS 16

Another notable source of information on Paul and women in the early church is his greetings to co-workers. Toward the end of most of his letters, Paul greets those to whom he is writing or sends greetings to those people from his associates. The longest of these greeting passages is Romans 16. Romans is, itself, Paul's longest, weightiest, and historically most influential letter. It was probably written between 54 and

58 A.D., apparently from Corinth, where Paul awaited an opportunity to go to Jerusalem and then on to Spain, unevangelized territory. For that project, he needed the spiritual and material support of the Roman church.

As is the pattern in the authentic Pauline letters, Romans closes with personal greetings, although it is a puzzle how Paul might have known so many people in a church he had yet to visit. Chapter 16 lists a large number of names, and scholars disagree on exactly how many and which are males and which females. Schüssler Fiorenza argues that there are twenty-six persons mentioned by name in the chapter, of whom a third are women; seven of them are mentioned by name. Careful reading suggests an almost exact balance in the order in which women and men are named and reveals that the range of roles for women is greater than that given for men. Two of the highest positions in the early church, deacon and apostle, are granted to named women in the chapter.

Before discussing the two women leaders, however, some textual issues connected with the chapter should be noted. The doxology and blessing, 16:25–27 and 16:20 in our translations, appear in different places in different of the ancient manuscript traditions of Romans. Some manuscripts reproduce chapters 1–14 and 16:25–27, some chapters 1–15 and 16:25–27, and some end at 16:23. Marcion's text omits chapters 15 and 16 altogether. Scholarship proposes at least three major solutions to the problem of the text. First, some scholars conclude that the text as it is reproduced in modern editions of the New Testament is the text as Paul wrote it (for there is no question that Romans is authentically Pauline). Second, some students of Paul suggest that Romans 16 is an independent piece of Pauline correspondence which was placed here when the letters were edited. Since Paul lived in Ephesus longer than anywhere else, it is argued that Romans 16 was actually addressed to that church. Or, since Tertullian notes that in an early collection of Paul's letters Romans came last, chapter 16 might have been viewed as an impressive ending for the whole corpus. Finally, Romans 16 is sometimes thought not to have been a part of the original Pauline collection at all but to be a later addition to the letter intended to bind Paul more closely to the Roman church. Perhaps the best short description of this perplexing textual problem is found in C. K. Barrett's *Epistle to the Romans* (1957; reprint, London: A. & C. Black, 1984). Barrett concludes his summary by noting that the problem will probably never be satisfactorily resolved, but that it in no way affects the substance of the epistle. Thus, insofar as chapter 16 presents an early Pauline view of the church and its workers, the textual issue does not substantially affect what it reveals about Paul and women in the early New Testament period.

The list of functional roles assumed by women in Roman 16 is impressive and includes deacon, protectress (patron), fellow worker, hard worker, and apostle. Of the women mentioned, only three—the mother of Rufus (v. 13), Julia, and the sister of Nereus (v. 15)—have no specific role mentioned in connection with them. The variety of terms used to describe the work done in the early church to which the chapter is addressed is not sex-specific; that is, both men and women seem to have assumed the various leadership roles mentioned in that church.

In his article cited earlier in this chapter, "Paul and His Co-Workers," E. Earl Ellis notes that, in descending frequency when Paul mentions fellow workers he notes co-workers (*synergos*, often with the implication of an itinerant ministry), "brethren," or "brothers and sisters" (NRSV *adelphos*, colleagues in religious work, the church as a whole), deacons (*diakonos*, a special class of co-workers active in preaching and teaching, a charismatic function with peripatetic implications), and apostles (*apostolos*, sometimes called "the Twelve," but in Paul's mind a wider, though still restricted group of leaders among whom he insists on numbering himself). Three of the four terms Paul uses for his co-workers are applied to women in Romans 16, and the fourth implies the inclusion of women. Prisca (v. 3) is a fellow worker, as apparently are Mary (v. 6) and Tryphaena and Tryphosa (v. 12). Phoebe (v. 1) is a deacon; Junia (v. 7) is an apostle, and all are "brethren" in the work of the church.

It would be remiss not to note that at this early stage in the church's history ministry was charismatic and not institutional. Leadership was a function of "gift," not "office." The New Testament does not reflect a cultic "priesthood," or any clearly defined office of sacerdotal responsibility. "Ministers" were those who assisted Jesus, the apostles, or those who had a specific duty to perform for the community. Ministry was an attitude of service before it was an office, and according to Christian parenesis (ethical exhortation) that attitude was to characterize all Christian people. When we talk about roles in the Pauline churches we are dealing with a hybrid combination of servanthood and leadership, not with "offices" as they later developed. With that in mind, what can we learn about the two prominent women servant leaders mentioned in Romans 16?

Romans 16:1–2 contains a wealth of information about Phoebe. The opening phrase, "I commend to you our sister Phoebe," is standard in letters of commendation at the time. Paul is providing an introduction to Phoebe so that she will receive hospitality of the kind which he, himself, had received from Lydia (see Acts 16:11–15). The *Didache,* a Christian teaching manual of the second century, reports that itinerant Christians were common, and it gives rules for discerning the "true" ones. Paul is assuring the recipients of the letter that Phoebe is bona fide. She is given recommendation in the same manner as Timothy in 1 Cor. 16:10–11.

If Romans 16 is actually part of the letter to Rome as Paul composed it, this commendation implies that Phoebe is, herself, carrying Paul's message to Rome. She is from Cenchreae, the port city of Corinth on the Sardonic Gulf. Since it is probable that Paul wrote Romans from Corinth, Phoebe might well be carrying his letter. If so, it points to women who served the church in itinerant capacities in its earliest days. (Recall the women of Luke 8:1–3, who will be discussed in chapter 5 of this study, and Euodia and Syntyche, who in Philippians were called "co-workers," with its implication of itinerancy.) Because ancient inns and hostels were notorious infestations of brigands and prostitutes, Phoebe would have been in some danger as carrier of the letter and was, thus, especially dependent on the hospitality of fellow-Christians as she traveled.

The name Phoebe is mythological and suggests that she was a freedwoman. In the text, she is defined not by her gender but by her ecclesial functions. Two technical terms describe the nature of Phoebe's work in her church. She is "deacon of the church" (*diakonon tēs ekklēsias*) and "helper of many" (*prostatis pollōn*). Both phrases are significant. "Deacon" is variously translated "servant," "helper," "minister," "deacon," and "deaconess" (in its feminine form). During the New Testament period, the meaning of the term in relation to an office is not self-evidently clear; the role was in the process of being defined and fixed. C. R. Meyer argued that Rom. 16:1 and 1 Tim. 3:8ff. and 5:9–13 provide evidence that deaconesses were ordained in the early church. On the basis of this evidence alone, I think Meyer overstates the case, but as "deacon" is applied by Paul to Phoebe it is hard to imagine anything other than an official function of some sort, probably a pastoral assistant who had helped Paul in his missionary work. Requirements and duties of the office of deacon are described in 1 Tim. 3:8–13, which was written some fifty to seventy years after Romans and by a disciple of Paul. Verse 11 of that passage does, however, indicate that women were deacons in their own right. Conservative translations and interpretations of the Greek text have obscured these women deacons and made them the wives of the male deacons even though the Greek word for "wife" is absent from the passage (see chapter 6 of this study). 1 Timothy is a much later work than Romans; however, the dual witness of the epistles, as well as the letter of Pliny the Younger which dates from about 112 A.D. and discusses two female slaves called "deacons" who were tortured to find out about the Christian community, would indicate that women served the church in that capacity.

The work of a female deacon probably would have been analogous to that of the male deacon. She would have served the Christian community, visited the poor, instructed the women and assisted at their baptisms, and interceded with the church authorities. The classic work, Philip Schaff's *History of the Christian Church* (1910), suggests that deaconesses held a regular office of self-denying charity and devotion to the welfare of the church. Although Phoebe is the only female deacon mentioned by name in the New Testament, her official capacity is confirmed by 1 Tim. 3:11, by parallel literature, and by the body of scholarly opinion about the technical term used to describe her here in Romans.

The phrase "helper of many" (*prostatis pollōn*) is the Greek equivalent of the Latin *patrona*. It is a *hapax legomenon* (a word occurring only once) in the New Testament. The usual meaning of the word is "leader," "president," "superintendent," or "patron" (see the verb form of the word in 1 Thess. 5:12 and 1 Tim. 3:4–5; 5:17). Probably the term meant "patroness," so that Phoebe, like Lydia in Acts 16, may have been a woman of enough wealth and social position to care for a church. She would have been patron of her community and, as such, would have represented the church in dealings with the government or the courts.

The feminine form of the word occurs in the Septuagint, where, in general, it is used for stewards of the king's property or for the chief officers over the people (see 1 Chron. 27:31; 2 Chron. 8:10; 24:11; 1 Esdras 2:12; Sirach 45:24; 2 Macc. 3:4.) A masculine form of the word is used three times in *1 Clement*, each time referring to Jesus as the guardian of Christians. The German scholar Martin Hengel has made mention of an unpublished Hebrew inscription in which a woman named Jael from Aphrodisias is a *prostatēs*, a word that, as I have indicated, had a technical-legal sense in the Greco-Roman patronage system. Whatever the exact meaning of the term, it suggests that Phoebe had helped many persons in the church, including Paul himself.

What, then, can we conclude about Phoebe and her role in the early church? She was a Christian highly recommended by Paul. She moved from place to place, possibly carrying Paul's letter to the church at Rome and was anxious to be with other Christians in her travels. She apparently held office in the church at Cenchreae, a church she served, worked in, and supported. Thus, about 60 A.D. one of the prominent apostolic churches had a woman deacon of whom its founder knew and approved. Phoebe was Paul's Christian sister in spite of her Gentile background, a full member of the Christian family. While there may have been different roles and ministries in the church, there was only one "status," that of brothers and sisters in Christ. Since no husband is mentioned in connection with her, we may conclude that Phoebe either is one of the "virgins" to whom Paul referred in 1 Corinthians 7 or is a widow who took on special (and even dangerous) tasks on behalf of the church.

In addition to the general textual problem mentioned in connection with Romans 16, v. 7 has a particular problem. Is the second person named male or female? The witnesses of the major English translations are as follows: KJV, Junia; RSV, Junias; NAS, Junias (with a note "or Junia, fem."); NEB, Junias (with a note "or Junia some witnesses Julia or Julias); NAB, Junia; NIV, Junias; NRSV, Junia. What we are dealing with is a textual variant that Bruce Metzger calls a "clerical error" (*A Textual Commentary on the New Testament* [London: United Bible Societies, 1975], 539). Some texts have *Iounian* and some *Ioulian*. The main argument against this person being female is the description "of note among the apostles." Translators reasoned that since a woman couldn't be an apostle, the person here called an apostle couldn't be a woman.

Several recent scholarly works, chief among them a 1977 article by Bernadette Brooten, argue that such reasoning begs the question; these recent works accept the textual variant "Julia" and the natural reading "Junia," concluding that she is, indeed, female. This "recent" rendering of the text is supported by the witnesses of the earliest commentators on Romans. Origen of Alexandria (ca. 185–233), the first commentator on the passage, understood a woman to be named here.

So did Jerome (340–420) and John Chrysostom (344–407), who remarked:

> to be an apostle is something great. But to be outstanding among the apostles—just think what a wonderful song of praise that is! They were outstanding on the basis of their works and virtuous actions. Indeed, how great the wisdom of this woman must have been that she was even deemed worthy of the title apostle.

Apparently no commentator until Aegidius of Rome (1245–1316) took the name to be masculine. Further, modern philologists note that "Junias" is, to date, unattested in Greek or Latin inscriptions and literature. It is a name that seems not to have existed in the period.

While I cannot settle the debate conclusively here, I am convinced by the historical commentary and the textual evidence that Junia was a female. Conjecturally, then, what would that imply? First, we would have another husband and wife team like Prisca and Aquila of Corinth (v. 3). Missionary partnership seems to have been common, and it is logical that many such partners would have been married couples. Second, both husband and wife were imprisoned with Paul and were Christians before he was. Perhaps this means that they were part of the circle of Jerusalem apostles who received a vision of the risen Lord (1 Cor. 15:7). As "kinsmen," they were fellow Jews, again like Prisca and Aquila. Third, both were "noteworthy" among the apostles in the obvious sense "noteworthy apostles within the larger group of those called apostles." And this lends strong evidence to the case that Paul's thinking and mission included female apostles. As Elisabeth Schüssler Fiorenza notes, when people joined the early Christian missionary movement, they joined an association of equals.

Like the term "deacon," the term "apostle" is not self-defining. Luke and Paul use the term differently in their writings. (Paul, for example, would not have met the Lukan criteria for apostleship given in Acts 1:21–22.) However, "apostle" is generally understood to include persons who had had a vision of the risen Christ and who were given a charge of some sort. It referred to a restricted group in the leadership of the church. Paul jealously claimed this title for himself and asserted its primacy (see, for example, 1 Cor. 1:1; Gal. 1:1; Rom. 1:1–6). If Junia were a woman (and there is strong evidence for this), then she was an authorized evangelist, one "sent" (Greek *stellō*). The role of the apostle was of particular importance because it involved the question of who had authority in the early church. The term in the New Testament did not refer to a closed circle from a past time (the "Twelve," for example) or to a function that could not be repeated, and this has massive implications for ecclesiology. But that is not our subject.

In addition to Phoebe and the missionary couple Andronicus and Junia, Paul greets Prisca (Priscilla) and Aquila, whose prominence is indicated by the fact that they appear first in a list of greetings. In four of six New Testament texts mentioning them, Prisca's name comes first, which suggests her prominence, or higher social status than her husband, or both. Acts 18 mentions the pair as having been expelled from Rome when Claudius expelled the Jews (49 A.D.). They had already taken up residence in Corinth when Paul arrived there, and they moved with him to Ephesus, where they established a house-church (1 Cor. 16:19). In Ephesus they met Apollos, and it was apparently Priscilla who instructed him in "the way of God" (Acts 18:26). Paul also sends greetings to Mary, "who has worked very hard among you" (v. 6) and to "those workers in the Lord, Tryphaena and Tryphosa" and "the beloved Persis, who has worked hard in the Lord" (v. 12). These women too are apparently leaders in their community.

The text of Romans 16 provides evidence of the important roles women fulfilled in the spread of Christianity in its earliest days. Unfortunately this text has been overlooked, misinterpreted, and poorly translated. What it suggests is that women performed the same named functions as men in important churches of Paul's acquaintance.

BIBLIOGRAPHY

[Committee on the Role of Women in Early Christianity of the Catholic Biblical Association]. "Women and the Priestly Ministry: The New Testament Evidence." *CBQ* 41 (1979): 613.

Brooten, B. "Junia . . . Outstanding Among the Apostles." In *Women Priests*, edited by L. and A. Swidler. New York: Paulist, 1977.

_____. *Women Leaders in the Ancient Synagogue*. Chico, Calif.: Scholars Press, 1982.

Goodspeed, E. "Phoebe's Letter of Introduction." *HTR* 44 (1951): 56.

Meyer, C. R. "Ordained Women in the Early Church." *Chicago Studies* 4 (1965): 285–308.

Schüssler Fiorenza, E. "Missionaries, Apostles, Coworkers: Romans 16 and the Reconstruction of Women's Early Christian History." *Word and World* 4 (1986): 420–33.

Thomas, W. D. "Phoebe: A Helper of Many." *ExpTms* 95 (1984): 336–37.

CONCLUSIONS

If this chapter has demonstrated nothing else, I hope it indicates something of the complexity of trying to abstract from the biblical text Paul's general view of women. The issue of women is not unlike any other issue, theme, or idea for which we might consult Pauline writings to determine his views. What was Paul's view of God or righteousness or eating meat offered to idols or of men as leaders of Christian communities? Paul addresses such subjects in several letters and with several communities in mind. He did not write systematic treatises, but occasional correspondence. It might be more honest and accurate to survey the range of things Paul says about a topic rather than to assert that we know his one, definitive view of that topic.

Second, in this chapter we have looked at only some, although I hope representative, passages that deal with women in the authentic Pauline corpus. It could be argued that the selection of these texts skews the view of Paul on the subject of women. Certainly selection and editing involve decision making. I have not intentionally omitted genuinely Pauline texts that seemed to me negative toward women, and I have tried to present a variety of kinds of material that exists in the Pauline corpus. Paul was a man of his time. His approach to all the issues he addresses is androcentric. And yet I am not aware of any specific authentically Pauline passage where Paul criticizes women as women, limits their role in the church because they are women (he may limit them for cultural reasons, but this is a slightly different issue), or indicates repugnance in the face of women's leadership in the church communities that he founded and/or visited.

This is not to say that Paul is a "feminist." I would be very hesitant to apply a twentieth-century term to a first-century person. What I, personally, see in Paul as he is reflected in his letters is a man in process, a person struggling to understand the full implications of what God has done in Jesus and what, specifically, that means for him. Paul was living the tension between what had *been* his tradition and what was coming to *be* his tradition. As a result, as Constance Parvey noted in "The Theology and Leadership of Women in the New Testament," we get "mixed messages" from Paul with regard to women. On the one hand he asserts a theology of the equality of men and women in Christ (as in Gal. 3:28), and on the other hand he suggests practices that, in their interpretation by the churches, led to the subordination of women (as, for example, the passages in 1 Corinthians). On the theological level, Paul has a vision of equality, but on the practical level he often practices a status quo ethic.

Paul came to understand that the gospel of Jesus Christ broke down traditional barriers in his society. The "barrier" of gender is but one example of the wider issue for Paul. One way to put the matter is to say, with Elaine Pagels, that Paul had a vision of human liberation but that he was unable to sustain it without ambivalence. And considering his own background, we should not be surprised by that fact. Paul does envision new possibilities for women and for slaves, but he does not challenge the social structures that perpetuated their domination. To that degree, Paul was a good Roman citizen. He feared social disorder and attempted to limit it by means of the instructions he gave to his churches. It seems to me that in the Pauline churches it was these injunctions that the subsequent generation of leaders fixed on. The Deutero-Pauline writings attempt to reinterpret Paul for a "new generation." And that later generation, for whom disorder in the Christian assembly and challenge to the dominant social order presented special problems, backed away from Paul's theoretical understandings but embraced his practical injunctions, with unfortunate results for Christian women, as we shall see in chapter 6 on the Deutero-Pauline writings.

Finally, then, I don't know that I could assert that Paul's teaching and practice with regard to women were "radically egalitarian," but neither would I call Paul "misogynistic" or "anti-woman." The evidence from major genuinely Pauline epistles like 1 Corinthians, Philippians, Galatians, and Romans suggests that Paul did not censor women who held leadership positions in the churches that existed before he began his missionary work, and that he did work side by side with and appreciate the ministry of women in the churches he founded. When he gives prescriptions with regard to women they are usually in the larger context either of church order or of the church's "reputation" in its society, and in those passages we see Paul torn between the gospel theology of equality and the established customs of his own age and culture. Paul, it seems to me, did not fully understand the implications of his abstract theological positions for social change. Unfortunately, Christian tradition seems not to have understood that Paul, as brilliant a thinker and as energetic a missionary as he was, had not fully integrated the radical implications of the gospel he proclaimed. As a result, tradition has attributed to Paul firm positions on a variety of subjects, including that of the place of women in the church, which, in my estimation, he did not hold. Paul struggled, as all serious Christians do, with the call of Christ and the demands of culture, with the idealistic (some would say radical) teachings of Jesus on the kingdom of God and the status quo of "acceptable norms." Let the one who is without conflict in this arena cast the first stone at Paul.

BIBLIOGRAPHY

Pagels, E. "Paul and Women: A Response to Recent Discussion." *JAAR* 42 (1974): 538–49.

Parvey, C. "The Theology and Leadership of Women in the New Testament." In *Religion and Sexism,* edited by Rosemary Radford Ruether, 139–46. New York: Simon & Schuster, 1974.

4

The Gospels: Mark and John

INTRODUCTORY ISSUES

A DISCUSSION OF WOMEN IN THE GOSPELS or of Jesus and women raises more of the difficult problems in the study of the New Testament, literary questions about gospel as a genre of literature and the historical Jesus debate. It will be important at least to introduce these two issues before turning to our subject.

One difficulty with defining "gospel" is that a single word is used two ways. "Gospel" is both the oral proclamation of the early Christians (the content of that proclamation) and a literary form "invented," or at least "adapted," by them. As C. S. Mann notes in his introduction to the Gospel of Mark, the gospel "is the message that God's righteous purposes for Israel have reached both goal and climax in and through the ministry of Jesus" (*Mark*, Anchor Bible [Garden City, N.Y.: Doubleday, 1986], 3). The earliest use of the "gospel" (*to euaggelion*) is connected with verbs of speaking and responding, not writing and reading. The verb form in Greek is related to the Hebrew *biśśar*, "to announce news of salvation." "Gospel" is used in Greek literature in the context of "reward for bringing good news" and also the good news itself; "gospel" is found in reports of good news of a victory and of the announcing of the birth of a king/emperor.

In the Christian context, "gospel" referred to the content of the oral message which proclaimed God's saving action in Jesus. The pivotal point of that message is that Jesus is the expected Messiah. Paul is the first New Testament writer to use the term, and its content is summarized by him in 1 Cor. 15:1–8 and Rom. 1:16–17. Luke gives us the substance of gospel proclamation in the sermons he places in the mouth of Peter (see, e.g., Acts 2:14–39). Mark 1:14–15 says that Jesus himself preached the "gospel of God." So "gospel" as proclamation is primarily concerned with God's action; God is the primary actor in gospel.

All of the genuine letters of Paul were apparently written before any of the literary works we call gospels (see chapter 3). They evince slight interest in the "biography" of Jesus. After the fall of Jerusalem (70 A.D.), the focus on Jesus himself developed. Attention shifted from God's action *in and through* Jesus (Paul's primary concern) to the person *of* Jesus; in the words of Rudolf Bultmann's famous dictum, "the proclaimer became the proclaimed." But this does not make gospels biographies. While they are related to the Greco-Roman genres of aretalogy and popular biography and to Jewish "biographies of the prophets," they do not mirror those forms exactly. (For a helpful discussion of genre, see David Aune, *The New Testament in its Literary Environment* [Philadelphia: Westminster, 1987], chapter 1, "The Genre of the Gospels.")

As a Christian literary genre, a gospel is a brief, popular writing in the language of the common people that probably arose outside Palestine in Gentile regions. Its purpose was as propaganda for the early Christian movement. Gospels contain historical reminiscences of Jesus and his ministry; but their use was to be evangelistic, and their interest was religious, not strictly historical or biographical in the modern sense of those terms. The aim of gospels, as John 20:31 asserts, is to evoke and strengthen faith in Jesus the Christ: "these are written so that you may come to believe that Jesus is the Messiah, the Son of God, and that through believing you may have life in his name." Certainly the center of a gospel is Jesus of Nazareth, but its primary concern is not facts *about* him but faith *in* him.

The gospels were written by people more interested in a living Lord present in their midst than in Jesus the historical man from Nazareth. Many scholars now hold that much of what is placed on the lips of Jesus in the Gospels was put there by Gospel writers (just as the writers of Hellenistic history placed speeches on the lips of famous persons). It is really the understanding that Gospels are faith documents that has led to what is called the "quest of the historical Jesus."

Recognizing the complexity of the sources for a life of Jesus, scholars in the last two hundred years have tried to go behind the "surface" of the Gospels to arrive at a historical picture of Jesus of Nazareth "as he really was." (For discussions of the first stages of the quest, see A. Schweitzer, *The Quest of the Historical Jesus* [New York: Macmillan, 1956]; and J. M. Robinson, *A New Quest of the Historical Jesus and Other Essays* [Philadelphia: Fortress, 1983].) Using form and redaction criticism and other methods of "higher criticism," the attempt has been made to find the "authentic Jesus material" in the Gospels. A most controversial recent manifestation of the quest has been the Jesus Seminar of the Society of Biblical Literature, which has produced at least a dozen major studies on Jesus, an edition of the Gospels color coded to reflect their estimation of the historical authenticity of the material, and a flurry of activity in the popular press. (For examples of the Jesus Seminar writing, see Marcus J. Borg, *Jesus: A New Vision* [New York: Harper & Row, 1987]; and John Dominic Crossan, *The Historical Jesus* [San Francisco: HarperSanFrancisco, 1991]. Representative of opposition to the Seminar's approach is Luke T. Johnson, *The Real Jesus* [New York: HarperCollins, 1995].)

In the last twenty years Jesus has been described as an eschatological prophet, a political revolutionary, a magician, a Pharisee, an Essene, a Galilean charismatic, and a Galilean rabbi. The titles applied to him in the Gospels (Son of Man, Son of God, Lord, Messiah/Christ) have been discussed and rediscussed. The issue for us is how the question of the historical Jesus affects our understanding of women as they are presented in the New Testament.

First, it necessitates what Elisabeth Schüssler Fiorenza has called a "hermeneutic of suspicion." When we read Gospel stories, we can no longer assume that they represent an objective picture of what Jesus said or did. Our Gospel texts reflect the points of view of the people writing them and the communities for which they were written. This is not to say the stories are "made up." On the contrary, in my estimation they do contain historical material; and the more unusual the behavior of Jesus is vis-à-vis women, the more likely the stories are to be grounded in a historical reality. We must ask, however, why an evangelist preserved a given story or saying, since the evangelists clearly edited and selected their materials from a far greater pool of material than what appears in the Gospels. (Again, John the evangelist admits as much. "Now Jesus did many other signs in the presence of his disciples, which are not written in this book" [John 20:30].) What was the significance of a given account for the evangelist's community? Why was it important to tell this story in this context? These are important questions for an understanding of what the Gospels say about and to women.

Second, then, we must bear in mind that the canonical Gospels as we have them (and there are, of course, noncanonical gospels with very different views of Jesus) present the first-century churches' reflections on their recollections of Jesus. Those early church communities grew and flourished in patriarchal surroundings like those described in chapter 1. The social setting of the communities influenced the viewpoints set forth in the Gospels (as a redaction-critical study of practically any pericope (an individual unit of material or "story") in the Synoptic Gospels will attest). This means that the best way to understand what Gospels say about and to women is to look at each Gospel separately in its own historical context so far as we are able to recreate it.

In the material that follows, then, we will be looking first at the view of women in the Gospel of Mark and then in the Gospel of John. Mark is probably the first Gospel to be written and therefore provides a particularly interesting point of departure, and since John is the last of the canonical Gospels to be composed it brings the Jesus material full cycle. Matthew and Luke's Gospels represent the "middle stage" of Gospel writing. Luke-Acts is treated in a separate chapter. Primarily for reasons of space, Matthew is omitted from this study. Women are least in evidence in Matthew's Gospel, which, in fact, has the fewest mentions of women. In Matthew, women are most likely to appear in ways that conform to Jewish customs and expectations at the end of the first century. This, in itself, is significant. Because women are marginalized in Matthew and because there has been little scholarly attention to the question of women in Matthew, it will be an important study for someone to undertake. And we should bear in mind that the more positive pictures in Mark, John, and Luke-Acts need to be balanced by the Matthean view.

Within any given Gospel there are at least two kinds of material on women. First, there is narrative material, stories that deal with Jesus' encounter with women. Second, there are the teachings of Jesus, discourses, parables, sayings, which directly mention women or reflect Jesus' attitude toward them (or at least the evangelist's view of it). In the discussion that follows I shall try to make use of both.

WOMEN IN THE GOSPEL OF MARK

Like all Gospels, Mark, the earliest canonical Gospel, is a popular
work intended to evoke faith that Jesus is the Messiah and Son of God.
One way to read Mark is as what is technically known as a "folktale,"
a realistic narrative with particularizing detail that is meant to be read
aloud to hearers, much as a story would be told. In his discussion of
Mark in *The Literary Guide to the Bible* (Cambridge, Mass.: Harvard
University Press, 1987), John Drury notes that Mark's story was first
told among "unofficial people" who delighted that it said nothing good
about officialdom—Roman, Jewish, or apostolic. Where this popular
story originated is one of the great puzzles of contemporary New Testament scholarship.

The scholarly consensus is that before the Gospel of Mark was written there existed an oral proclamation of Jesus, probably a written
account of his passion, a number of "narrative complexes" (collections
of narratives of the same literary type, for example, parables or miracle
stories), and a collection of Jesus sayings called "Q," although it is
unclear whether or not Mark had access to that collection. In the Q
material, Jesus uses feminine images in the proclamation of his message (Luke 7:35; 13:34), foresees special difficulties for his female followers (Luke 12:53; 14:26), and seeks to protect the rights of women in
divorce proceedings. Since Q must be reconstructed from Matthew
and especially Luke, I am cautious of speculating too much about Q's
view of women.

A complex of factors led to the writing of Gospels in the second half
of the first century. The expected return of Jesus in glory was delayed,
and the eyewitnesses of his ministry were dying or being martyred in
the first organized persecutions of Christians as Christians. Within the
church there was increasing need for a standardized version of Jesus'
life and teachings both to answer questions of authority and to serve
as a missionary tool in the Gentile mission. Gospels were written to
answer these needs.

Mark was probably written between 65 and 75 A.D.; most scholars
think it was before the destruction of the Temple in 70 A.D., since its
destruction does not seem to be reflected in the text. Toward the end
of Nero's reign (54–68 A.D.) Christians in Rome suffered terrible persecutions. Apocalyptic expectations surged with the Jewish War of 66–70

A.D. Both of these facts are reflected in Mark, which seems to have been written for a church undergoing suffering. The most ancient traditions associate the Gospel of Mark with the apostle Peter and the city of Rome. Eusebius's *Ecclesiastical History* (3.39) quotes Papias (ca. 140 A.D.), who notes that Mark was "Peter's interpreter." Although the Greek and Latin fathers to St. Jerome in the fifth century associate Mark's Gospel with Peter, modern scholars doubt the connection.

The Roman provenance of the Gospel is debated, but some contemporary scholars support Rome as the location of the writing. That Mark explains both Jewish customs and the Aramaic expressions he retains suggests at the very least a primarily Gentile audience. Mark contains many Latin loanwords, which would support a Roman location, except that most of the loanwords are military terms and, therefore, might have come from any place in the Empire. That Matthew and Luke both used Mark in writing their Gospels suggests that it came from a well-known Christian center. Other locations that have been suggested for the writing of Mark include Palestine generally, Galilee, and Syria just north of Galilee.

At best we can conclude only that the Gospel of Mark was written primarily for Gentile readers in some unspecified part of the Empire. Mark's community, then, was predominantly but not exclusively Gentile. They did not observe Mosaic law and had known or were about to experience persecution. This accounts for the heavily apocalyptic tone of the work. As James Hoover's study guide for Mark notes, theologically and pastorally, Mark retells the Jesus story to show that the kingdom in its glory comes at the end of a path of suffering and service (*Mark: Follow Me* [Downers Grove, Ill.: InterVarsity, 1985], 8). As is the case with all the Gospels, the writer is unknown (although traditionally associated with the John-Mark of Acts), but wrote in rough Greek from a location central enough that his Gospel was well known and foundational for the writing of subsequent Gospels.

Turning now to Markan stories about Jesus and women and Jesus' teachings that deal with women, we must bear in mind the effect that the Markan community would have had on that material. First, the accounts reflect the Jewish culture and Palestinian background of the characters *in* the story. Second, the stories were probably written in a more cosmopolitan setting than the one in which they occurred. If, for example, the women of Mark's community are Roman, they would have had relatively more legal and social freedoms than the women they encounter in the Gospel stories. Third, these are the first written stories we have that describe Jesus' behavior and attitude toward women.

Mark and John have roughly the same proportion of women characters to men; about one-fourth of the persons in those Gospels are women. In the sixteen chapters of Mark there are thirteen pericopae in which women are central to the narrative: 1:30–31; 3:31–35; 5:21–24, 35–43; 5:24–34; 6:3; 6:14–29; 7:24–30; 12:41–44; 14:3–9; 14:66–69; 15:40–41, 47; 16:1–8. In only five cases are the women referred to by their own names: Mary, Jesus' mother (6:3); Herodias, in the martyrdom of John the Baptist (6:19); Mary Magdalene, Mary the mother of James and Joses, and Salome at the cross (15:40); Mary Magdalene and Mary the mother of Joses, who saw where Jesus' tomb was (15:47); and Mary Magdalene, Mary the mother of James, and Salome at the empty tomb (16:1). (Mary Magdalene, Mary the mother of James and Joses, and Salome seem to parallel the male "inner circle" of Peter, James, and John elsewhere in Mark; see 5:37; 9:2; and 14:33.) The other women in the Gospel are designated either in relationship to men— Simon's mother-in-law (1:30); Jesus' mother and sisters (3:31–35; 6:3); Jairus's daughter (5:23); a widow (12:41–44); a servant girl of the high priest (14:66–69); and the previously noted Mary mother of Joses and James (15:40, 47; 16:1)—or to their nationality—a Syrophoenician woman (7:24–30). Only the woman with the flow of blood (5:24–34) and the anointing woman (14:3–9) stand independently in the Gospel.

While few women appear, and even fewer appear by name, it is important to remember that the many Markan "crowd scenes" would have been made up of both men and women. As noted in chapter 2 above, Jewish women in rural Palestine enjoyed a fair degree of freedom of movement. The woman healed of a hemorrhage in Mark 5 is evidence of this. Mark frequently makes reference to "people," "crowds," and "multitudes" (1:4–5, 32–34, 45; 2:1, 12; 3:7–12, 20; 4:1; 5:14; 6:30ff., 53–56; 7:14, 33, 37; 8:1–9; 9:14; 10:34, 46; 11:1–11; 15:8), and each would have included women. Thus, women would have experienced Jesus in his public role as miracle worker and teacher. They would have "been amazed," "followed," participated in the triumphal entry into Jerusalem and perhaps the call for Jesus' crucifixion. When we mentally picture these crowd scenes, it is important to picture them with women present.

Furthermore, Mark 15:40–41 notes that Mary Magdalene, Mary, and Salome "used to follow him and provided for him when he was in

Galilee." Significantly, "to follow" is a technical term for discipleship throughout the Gospel. The Greek form used in 15:41 for "follow" (*ēkolouthoun*) is the same word used for the responses of Andrew and Simon in 1:18 and Levi in 2:14, and the word for "provided" is probably more accurately translated "ministered" or "served" (*diēkonoun*), the term which describes the central aspect of Jesus' own ministry and that required of his disciples. In addition, Mark 15:41 notes that "there were many other women who had come up with him to Jerusalem" (compare Luke 8:1–3). This indicates that the original circle of Galilean disciples included women who perhaps were present when Jesus gave special instructions to disciples. Mark 4:10–34 (and 7:17; 9:28; 10:10) speaks of such private instruction—"those who were around him along with the Twelve" (4:10) and "he explained everything in private to his disciples" (4:34)—and makes clear that Jesus' inner circle included more than the Twelve. In fact "his disciples" (*tois idiois mathētais*) is used forty-three times in Mark for Jesus' followers and "the Twelve" only ten times. Thus, Mark 4:10 and 15:40–41 suggest that just as we must picture women in the "crowds" in Mark's Gospel, each time we encounter the term "disciples" women should perhaps be included in the group we picture.

In Mark's narrative the women disciples come off rather better than do the male followers of Jesus. It is a commonplace of Markan scholarship that the disciples in Mark are a sorry lot. The named male disciples misunderstand Jesus' person, mission, and teaching (see, e.g., 6:35–36; 6:49, 52; 8:16–21; 9:32–36; 10:35–45; 13:1); are personally sharp with him (4:38; 5:31; 8:4; 14:4); and disobey his commands (7:36). In the dramatic central scene of the Gospel, Mark 8:27–9:1, Peter confesses Jesus but completely misunderstands the meaning of his confession, as evidenced by his rebuke of the Lord in 8:32. One of Jesus' male disciples, Judas Iscariot, betrays Jesus to the religious authorities (14:10–22); at Jesus' arrest the male disciples flee (14:50–52); and while Jesus asserts before the council that he is, indeed, the Christ, Peter is busy denying him in the courtyard below (Mk 14:53–72). In Mark's Gospel, the only explicitly noted males around Jesus at the crucifixion are the soldiers who execute him; a passerby pressed into service to carry his cross, Simon of Cyrene; and a centurion at the foot of the cross.

In contrast, the women in the Gospel are, by and large, models of discipleship. Simon's mother-in-law "serves" (*diakonei*) when she is healed, the prototypical act of discipleship (1:30–31). The woman with a flow of blood has the faith necessary to approach Jesus (5:24–34). The Syrophoenician woman apparently "bests" Jesus in debate and teaches him something about the extent of his mission (7:24–30). An anonymous widow is an example of religious devotion and self-giving (12:41–44), and in a similarly generous act, an anonymous woman anoints Jesus in Bethany in a manner that leads him to speak of his impending martyrdom (14:3–9). In Mark's Gospel it is the faithful women disciples who witness the crucifixion (15:40–41), follow along to see where Jesus' body is buried (15:47), and set out early the first day of the week to anoint the body (16:1–8), thereby becoming the first witnesses to the resurrection and those charged with proclaiming it.

The fact that they do not immediately do so is especially noteworthy, since women to this point have been so positively portrayed by Mark. It has been noted that reporting the fear of the women is a standard literary device. Fear, awe, and wonder are standard features of the epiphany scenes in Hellenistic literature, and the fact that the women in 16:8 "said nothing to anyone" forms an interesting "inverted inclusion" with 1:44. There at the beginning of the Gospel, a leper who has been charged *not to* speak begins to "proclaim . . . freely." Here those charged *to* speak are silent. (At least initially, for, as we know, the news of the resurrection did circulate!) No disciples in Mark's Gospel are perfect. All are "in process," and the fact that Mark closes at 16:8 with the women's testimony in doubt shows just how fragile the gospel is. Will the reader respond to it, proclaim it, or simply remain silently "in fear"?

The fact that women appear in a positive light and are brought to the fore especially at the end of Mark's Gospel, where named women appear (only two appear by name until chapter 15 and both are depicted pejoratively—Mary the mother of Jesus and Herodias), especially illuminates the evangelist's view of discipleship. According to Mark, like John the Baptist, Jesus preached, was delivered up, and was martyred. Disciples are not greater than their masters. Disciples are to take up their crosses and follow, to lose their lives for the gospel (8:34–35), to be "last of all and servant of all" (9:35). In the Jewish ethos of the story itself, and the wider Greco-Roman culture in which it occurred and is recorded, for women to become prominent disciples and witnesses of Jesus is a prime example of the last becoming first. It is one of Mark's icons of the surprising social reality of the kingdom of God. As Winsome Munro noted, the rehabilitation of the Twelve and their future authority depend on their accepting the testimony of women.

It is not possible to treat each of the sixteen occurrences of women in Mark's Gospel in detail, but brief commentary on four accounts—the woman with the flow of blood (5:24–34), the Syrophoenician woman (7:24–30), the generous widow (12:41–44), and the anointing woman (14:3–9)—will give a fuller picture of the Markan community's understanding.

The account of the woman with the flow of blood (5:24–34) is particularly dramatic, since the woman is marginalized on four counts. She is female, without a male relative to be her advocate (we know this because she is not identified by male kin), without financial resources (she has spent her money on doctors—first-century gynecologists? [v. 26]), and she is subject to blood taboo. Leviticus 15:19–30 sets out the limitations on menstruating women. Not only is this woman considered "unclean"; she makes "impure" anything or anyone she touches. "A flow of blood" effectively meant that a woman could not leave home, not have intercourse with her husband or any normal social contact, much less any religious or cultic activity. In effect, this woman has been excluded by her society for twelve years. (See further Marla J. Selvidge, "Mark 5:25–34 and Leviticus 15:19–20: A Reaction to Restrictive Purity Regulations," *JBL* 103 [1984]: 619–23.)

This makes it startling that we do not find her in the seclusion of a home (where three of four major Markan healings occur). She had heard about Jesus (v. 27) and takes the initiative *to go to him* (unique in the healings of Mark). She violates both social custom (which would have prevented any woman from approaching and speaking to a male in public, much less an "impure" one) and blood taboo to go to Jesus. And in her "impure" state she dares to touch him, with the result that she is healed (v. 29). When Jesus asks who touched him and the (male?) disciples chide him for such a silly question in a crowd, although she could have disappeared in that crowd, the woman comes forward to confess to Jesus what she had done. Her attitude and posture as described in v. 33, however, suggest that she accepts the norms of the male honor/shame culture.

But Jesus' response to her is remarkable. First, he speaks to a woman in a public place, thereby in effect acknowledging her existence. Second, he calls her "daughter," including her as a kinswoman (an illustration of the "family" constituted in 3:31–35) and makes it clear that it is *her* faith that has made her well. She has "suffered many things" (v. 26, a phrase Mark uses only of her and of Jesus himself [8:31; 9:12]), but now through her initiative is made whole, restored both physically and to her community. She in fact shows Jairus, with whose story hers is intercalated (5:21–24, 35–43), the faith that he must have for his daughter's healing. Mark 5:24–34 depicts Jesus as breaking social and religious custom to liberate one bound by both by restoring her to wholeness of body and social functioning.

In the story of the Syrophoenician woman (7:24–30) it is, in effect, she who restores Jesus to his proper attitude! Jesus has moved from Galilee into the province of Syria (v. 24) and is in a private house. There he is approached by another unlikely person, a Gentile woman, of Greek heritage and Syrophoenician by birth. She is, in short, of the wrong sex, the wrong national/ethnic status (Greek), and the wrong racial/religious background (Syrophoenician—to Jews a racial term with unsavory religious connotations). She is apparently a single parent with a daughter, which, in itself, was viewed as a liability (daughters needed dowries), and this one is demon-possessed. Like the woman with the flow of blood, Mark introduces her without male connections, and like that woman she throws herself at Jesus' feet, approaching in faith, this time with an altruistic request on behalf of her daughter. However, the Syrophoenician woman approaches Jesus in a house, a more customary setting for reputable women than on the street in public. (Note that this account follows a section on food taboos. Is Jesus at table in the house? If so, then this story hearkens back to the preceding one on food taboos in Mark 7:1–23 and serves to show the widened table fellowship among the followers of Jesus.)

Jesus' response to her in v. 27 is one of the most troubling christological verses in the Synoptic Gospels. It reflects the contempt of the Jews for "heathens" and depicts Jesus as a thoroughly racist and uncaring figure. It is particularly troubling since Jesus has already healed an "outsider," the demoniac from the Decapolis (5:1–20). Some scholars have tried to soften the picture by arguing that the verse is of doubtful authenticity or by pointing out that the term for "dogs" is diminutive, but it seems to me that in preserving this early story Mark and his community are reflecting an astonishing candor. Here is the human Jesus. He has entered a house hoping to be left alone (7:24), but is pursued by a woman. He responds sharply, circumscribed by his own background, but she persists in her approach, replying with equal quickness and candor first, by agreeing with Jesus and addressing him as "Lord," the only time he is so addressed in Mark, and then by pointing out that when children (Jews) are fed, dogs (Gentiles) get the leftovers (v. 28). Jesus has taught that custom should not stand in the way of helping those in need (2:23–28; 3:1–6). Jesus (remembering his own words?) recognizes the accuracy and wisdom of her response and effects a long-distance healing by freeing her daughter from the demon. Apparently, rather than finding his ego bruised, Jesus is won over by the persistence, wit, and intelligence of a Gentile woman.

Certainly Mark wants to contrast the way the religious authorities have come to Jesus (7:1-23) with the way the woman has. They come with a closed, legalistic attitude; she comes empty-handed and without merit, but open to Jesus. And she is rewarded, as he shatters the wall between Jew and Gentile in granting her request for her daughter. But it is, of course, she who has pointed out the absolute necessity of doing so. The story is complete in vv. 25–30, and redaction critics suggest that v. 24 was added by Mark. Thus, while the Markan community probably preserved the story as part of its attempt to comprehend the Gentile mission of the church and the relation between Jews and Gentiles therein, the point is that the woman did not hesitate to approach Jesus, and he did not hesitate to learn from her. Sharon H. Ringe has pointed out that *the woman* ministers to Jesus, first, by witnessing to his ability as a worker of miracles and, second, by engaging with him in a way that allows *him* to move beyond taboos and boundaries. Ringe believes that the Syrophoenician woman frees Jesus to heal, to transcend the racist and sexist boundaries of his society. The Syrophoenician woman represents the courage of those who, having little to lose, act boldly in faith on behalf of others (S. Ringe, "A Gentile Woman's Story," in *Feminist Interpretation of the Bible*, edited by L. Russell [Philadelphia: Westminster, 1985], 65–72).

When we come to the account of the generous widow (12:41–44), we must be especially careful not to assume too much or to miss implications because of the familiarity of the story and the relatively uniform way in which it has been interpreted. First, it should be noted that several stories of a similar nature exist. This may be an instance in which a story *by* Jesus becomes a story *about* Jesus (see, e.g., *Leviticus Rabba* 3.5, which is quoted in D. E. Nineham, *The Gospel of St. Mark* [Baltimore: Penguin, 1963], 334–35). Second, the traditional reading of the pericope is that Mark is closing the contentious Temple teaching sequence (11:27–12:44) with a contrast between outward religious ostentation and inward religious conviction; the anonymous widow is presented in sharp contrast to the scribes in 12:38–40. She, with the anointing woman, is an example of faithful action. Her witness is especially powerful, since, as a widow, she is without the legal and economic protection of a husband. In Hebrew scripture, widows are the special objects of God's concern, because they are "disposable" in the world's view. Israel is frequently warned not to treat widows unjustly (see, e.g., Exod. 22:22–24; Deut. 24:17; 27:19; Jer. 22:3). The vulnerable and invisible widow (unlike the ostentatious and powerful scribes of vv. 38–39) gave "everything she had" to support the Temple.

And herein, as professors Elizabeth Struthers Malbon and Addison Wright have pointed out, is the problem (E. Malbon. "The Poor Widow in Mark and Her Poor Rich Readers," *CBQ* 53 [1991]: 589–604; A. Wright, "The Widow's Mite: Praise or Lament?—A Matter of Context," *CBQ* 44 [1982]: 256–65). If Jesus is against the scribes' devouring widows' houses (v. 40), how can he approve of what he sees here? Is v. 44 a word of praise for the woman or of lament over a religious system that would lead such a person to give away all she had? In the context of the Temple and the controversies Jesus has just experienced there, what are we to think of a religious system that would encourage a vulnerable person to sacrifice what security she had for its institutional manifestation? Isn't the offering backward? Shouldn't the Temple be giving to the widow? Note that the very next words from Jesus are a prediction of the destruction of that Temple (13:2). In her comments on this passage, Hisako Kinukawa notes that widows are typical victims of temple-centered religion. I would suggest that while Jesus approves of the woman's devotion and generosity, he can hardly have approved of the religious system that demanded her living of her. Its continued oppression of the poor may well be one of the reasons why Jesus predicts its destruction. And, as Kinukawa observes, this widow's silently bearing unjust systems may have influenced Jesus to give *his* whole life as she has given hers.

Chapter 13, the Markan apocalypse in which Jesus speaks of the end of the present order, is framed by stories of two anonymous and exemplary women in contrast to named and venal men (the scribes, Judas). That, in itself, is noteworthy, since the story of the anointing woman in Mark 14:3–9 occurs in other contexts in the other evangelists. (Luke, for example, puts it toward the beginning of Jesus' public ministry; see Luke 7:36–50.) In strong contrast to the plots against Jesus by men in 14:1–2 and 10–11, Mark depicts the extravagant love of a woman for him in 14:3–9. It was a story that was so important that it is one of the few that all four evangelists recount.

This second woman of exemplary action also approaches Jesus in a home, as he is reclining at table—in the house of "Simon the leper"

(v. 3). Jesus' followers routinely meet in private homes, not in the Temple or synagogue (see, e.g., 1:29; 2:1, 15; 7:24; 9:33; 14:3, 15, 17), and here Jesus has already broken a cultural and religious taboo in keeping table fellowship, apparently at a feast (they are *reclining* at table), with one whose disease would normally make him an outcast (see Leviticus 13 and 14). Mark says only that the woman "came [*ēlthen*] with an alabaster jar of very costly ointment of nard" (v. 3), not that she "came in off the street." It appears to be the case that she was *one of* the guests at dinner, another indication that gatherings of Jesus' disciples regularly included women. This is a most unusual dinner party, made up as it seems to be of social outcasts. Jesus apparently drew his circle of fellowship quite widely!

This anonymous woman (again, there is no mention of a male relative) anoints Jesus' head with an expensive perfume, one that cost nearly a year's wages. In the ancient Near East anointing of the head signified selection for a special task, like kingship or priesthood. In Israel's united kingdom period a primary function of the prophet was to anoint kings with oil. This anointing is the woman's symbolic confession of Jesus' status as the Christ (Messiah, or "anointed one"). The extravagance of the gesture offends some of the other diners. (One wonders if they are embarrassed that *they* have not thought to show any gesture of love for Jesus.) When they begin to grumble, ostensibly about wastefulness in the face of poverty, Jesus defends the woman's action (vv. 6–7). Helping the poor is an important and perennial task, but it does not replace acts of love for particular individuals.

Some scholars think the story originally ended at v. 7. If that is the case, then Mark has added vv. 8–9 as a foreshadowing of the crucifixion and an indication of the prominence of women in the early Christian community. In the Markan story, the woman appears in a prophetic office, is the first person to understand Jesus as the crucified Messiah ("she has anointed my body beforehand for burial" [v. 8]; anointing of dead bodies *was* "women's work"), and anticipates the spice-bearing women who are the first to go to the tomb (16:1–2).

While these four pericopae depict women in positive and exemplary roles, that is not universally the case in Mark. Jesus' own mother appears in questionable light in 3:31–35, at which time Jesus reconstitutes his "family": "whoever does the will of God is my brother and sister and mother" (v. 35). Again in 6:1–6, when those in Jesus' hometown question his ministry, they do so on the basis of knowing him as "the carpenter, the son of Mary" (v. 3). Since no mention is made of

Joseph, Mary has apparently become "head of the household." We shall have occasion to mention Mary again in connection with John's Gospel where she appears much more favorably. Had we only Mark's view of her, and not that of Luke and John, Marian devotion might never have developed.

Likewise, Herodias and her daughter are depicted in 6:14–29 as thoroughly unsavory women. Herod invites his daughter to dance for his dinner guests—to begin with, rather questionable behavior for a father. One can imagine what sort of dance she performed. When it pleases his guests, Herod promises to give her "whatever you ask me" (v. 23), and after consultation with her mother, she asks for John the Baptist's head on a platter. It is a grotesque scene in which none of the players are commendable. Herodias was a woman of wealth, power, and wickedness. She may represent a commonly held view of what happens when women are allowed to exercise influence in the public realm. In any case, she is not directly associated with Jesus or his followers, and is certainly not exemplary.

Generally speaking, though, the women in narrative passages in Mark's Gospel who are associated with Jesus are depicted very positively indeed. How do women appear in the discourses or teachings of Jesus? First, women as such were not of particular concern to Jesus. He says nothing theologically about women as women or men as men. (Nor, I think, does any gospel. That is, the sex of disciples is not an issue in the teaching of Jesus as the narrative passages would attest.) When Jesus mentions women in Mark, it is in a familial context, in their roles as wives and mothers.

Twice Jesus speaks about marriage. In Mark 10:2–12 the Pharisees approach Jesus to ask if a *man* may lawfully divorce his wife. They knew, of course, that it was perfectly legal for a man to put his wife away, and the more liberal Pharisaic parties supported his right to do so for infractions as trivial as a burned supper. Jesus appeals not to the letter but to the spirit of the law by referring the Pharisees to God's intention at creation. At creation man and woman were made for each other, and they should not divorce. Practically, this pronouncement would have protected wives from being "disposable." When Sadducees come to Jesus with a hypothetical case about levirate marriage (12:18–27), Jesus refuses to see the wife in their example as "property" to be shared among brothers, but instead appeals to the more substantive issue of the nature of resurrection life and of God's own being (vv. 25–27).

In his teaching on family, we have already noted that Jesus viewed his family, "brother and sister and mother" (3:35), as those who did the will of God. And he notes that no one who loses biological family for his sake will not receive a "hundredfold now in this age . . . brothers and sisters, mothers and children, and . . . persecutions . . ." (10:30). Women are included in the family of Jesus constituted by obedience to God, and they are included in the persecutions he foresees for that family. In chapter 13, where Jesus speaks most directly of the trials that disciples will face at the end (which in 13:8 he calls "birthpangs"), he is especially concerned for women: "woe to those who are pregnant and to those who are nursing infants in those days!" (13:17). Jesus' words indicate a sensitivity to the reality of most women's experience in his day, the experience of being wife and mother.

In Mark's Gospel women appear prominently. They move from being the passive recipients of miracles, to being active examples of faithful response, to being given an apostolic commission to "go and tell his disciples and Peter" (16:7), a commission whose accomplishment Mark leaves ambiguous. According to Mark's understanding of discipleship—that it is a matter of following, serving, and suffering—women are prime examples. The women were not only capable of following, serving, and suffering, but in Mark's narrative did so more faithfully than the male disciples. Mary Ann Tolbert's conclusion, that Mark's community must have had strong women leaders and role models, is an appropriate one on the basis of the text of the Gospel as we have it. Written around 70 A.D. and compared to the prevailing attitudes of that period in the Greco-Roman world, Mark's Gospel represents an important shift in the positive value it assigns to women in the community of Jesus. Indeed, they are depicted as vital witnesses of the public ministry of Jesus, his death, and resurrection.

BIBLIOGRAPHY

Kinukawa, Hisako. *Women and Jesus in Mark: A Japanese Feminist Perspective.* Maryknoll, N.Y.: Orbis, 1994.

Malbon, Elizabeth S. "Fallible Followers: Women and Men in the Gospel of Mark." *Semeia* 28 (1983): 29–48.

Munro, Winsome. "Women Disciples in Mark?" *CBQ* 44 (1982): 225–41.

Schmitt, John J. "Women in Mark's Gospel." *Bible Today* 19 (1981): 228–33.

Schierling, M. J. "Women as Leaders in the Marcan Communities."
    Listening 15 (1980): 250–56.
Tolbert, Mary Ann. "Mark." In *The Women's Bible Commentary*,
    edited by C. Newsom and S. Ringe, 263–74. Louisville: Westmin-
    ster/John Knox, 1992.

WOMEN IN THE GOSPEL OF JOHN

The Gospel of John is the last of the canonical Gospels. Written about
90 A.D. and then edited by the community of its author about 100 A.D.
or shortly thereafter, it is one of the latest of the New Testament writings and evinces a development of Christian thought quite unlike that
of the earlier writings like Paul's letters or Mark's Gospel. John is a
deceptive Gospel. On the surface, its writing seems simple. Its Greek
is so uncomplicated that it is often used to teach that language to
beginning students. But behind the seemingly simple exterior is a
highly complex multicultural thought structure that resists the effort
to categorize it easily.

John tells the Jesus story quite differently from the Synoptic evangelists; 90 percent of John's material has no Synoptic parallel. In John,
Jesus' ministry is centered in Jerusalem rather than Galilee and lasts
three years rather than one. When events in the life of Jesus appear in
both John and the Synoptics, John may well have them in a different
context. For example, he places the Temple cleansing at the beginning
of Jesus' public ministry rather than at the end. The Synoptic Jesus
tells parables; the Johannine Jesus delivers discourses, often as a
response to a dialogue or miracle. In John there is no hint of Jesus'
earthly origins, no wilderness temptation, no exorcisms, no second-
coming predictions, no Last Supper, no agony in the garden.

This leads scholars to assume that John had different sources from
the Synoptic evangelists. His independent traditions probably
included what is referred to as a "signs source," a collection of sign
miracles, and it is unclear whether or not he depended literarily on the
Synoptics (as, say, Matthew depended on Mark). Older scholarship
tended to refer to John as the "Gospel for the Greeks," noting its use
of terms from Hellenistic philosophy, Gnosticism, the Hermetic literature and Mandaeanism. But John's thinking is also thoroughly Jewish.
The Gospel is structured around the feasts of Passover (2:23; 6:4;
11:56), Tabernacles (7:2), and Dedication or Hanukkah (10:22). John

exhibits thorough knowledge of Hebrew scripture and is familiar with disputes among groups of Pharisees and with the community at Qumran. And John has the best knowledge of all the evangelists of the details of the geography of Palestine and Jerusalem.

Who would have this sort of vast knowledge? Would that we knew. The traditional view is that John was John, the son of Zebedee who is mentioned in the Gospel. That seems to be born out by John 21:24, but there are other candidates from within the Gospel including John the Elder, John-Mark, Lazarus, and the equally enigmatic Beloved Disciple, whose influence was obviously strong in the community that produced this Gospel. The author of John was probably a Jew trained in the Diaspora synagogue who knew not only his own religious tradition, but had wide acquaintance with Hellenistic ideas and religions. He had excellent sources of information about Jesus and wrote good Greek. His gospel reflects the hostility between Christianity and the synagogue, which we know was evident in the 80s and 90s. He seems to be writing a theological interpretation of the Jesus story for readers already familiar with the details of that story. He wants to show Jesus as the fulfillment of Judaism and to delineate the Jesus community from that of the synagogue or of the followers of John the Baptist.

Since the name John has been associated with Ephesus, it is often speculated that the Gospel of John was written there. Certainly Ephesus would have the Jewish community and the religious and cultural pluralism reflected in the Gospel, and it was a well-known intellectual center from which to launch an interpretation of Jesus. Both Ignatius and Polycarp in the second century point to Asia Minor as the origin of John. Other proposals suggest that John was written in Alexandria, Antioch, Palestine, or somewhere in Syria. For our purposes, it should be noted that John probably arose in a highly cosmopolitan center, one in which women would have had varying degrees of freedom and cultural restriction. That is born out by the women we meet in the Gospel.

However, if a good deal of the ministry of Jesus in John occurs in Jerusalem rather than in Galilee, I am a little less prone to argue that we picture as many women in the "crowds" as we might in Mark's Gospel. There would certainly have been some, but in the "headquarters city" of Hellenistic Judaism, would women have been as free to move about the city as men? Would they have been as free as women in rural Galilee were by necessity? Wouldn't the religious laws and taboos that governed their lives have been more carefully enforced? If

Jesus taught in the Court of the Gentiles or of the Women when John depicts him as in the Temple, then there might be women in attendance. But if he were in more interior areas to which he as a Jewish male had access, then fewer women would have heard his teaching. I raise the issue tentatively, but it has influenced my thinking about the general picture of women in John's Gospel.

Certainly John raises up discipleship over apostleship. John never uses the term "apostle," and the term "disciple" does apply equally to men and women. There are seven scenes in John's Gospel in which women figure prominently. They occur in chapters 2, 4, 8, 11, 12, 19, and 20. In her article "Women in the Fourth Gospel and the Role of Women in the Contemporary Church," Sandra Schneiders makes four general points that serve well to introduce the overall picture of women revealed in those passages. (For the full article, see *Biblical Theology Bulletin* 12 [1982]: 35–45.) First, Schneiders notes that in John no woman is shown as resisting Jesus, failing to believe, deserting, or betraying him (compare with 3:10; 9:24–34; 12:4–6; 13:2, 27–30, 37–38; 16:18, 31–32; 18:1–11; 20:24–25). Second, the women characters in John are highly individuated, and women's religious experience is depicted as nuanced. This suggests the evangelist's experience of Christian women in his own community. Third, in John (as we saw in Mark), women are depicted as playing unconventional roles. The Samaritan woman in chapter 4 functions as an evangelist. In chapter 11 Martha seems to be conducting the funeral activity of her brother. Mary Magdalene ventures out alone at night (20:1). Furthermore, in John no woman but the mother of Jesus and Mary of Clopas is designated in relationship to a male, and women do not relate to Jesus by the mediation or permission of men. In fact, they are noted for their individual initiative and decisive action. John describes no "women's roles" that are different from those of the men around Jesus.

In the characterization of men and women in his Gospel, John frequently introduces representative types rather than named individuals. We meet, for example, a Samaritan woman in chapter 4, a paralytic in chapter 5, a woman caught in adultery (7:53–8:11, although as we shall note, the existence of this story in the oldest Johannine manuscripts is questioned), a man born blind (chapter 9). That the named women characters are limited more or less to Jesus' mother, Mary and Martha of Bethany, and the women at the cross (Jesus' mother and sister—whose names are not given—Mary the wife of Clopas, and Mary Magdalene [19:25]), does not mean that women were unimportant in the telling of Jesus' story. What should be noted is that John introduces male and female characters in the same way.

Following the pattern established in the discussion of Mark above, I shall survey briefly several Johannine texts dealing specifically with women (2:1–12; 4:1–42; 7:53–8:11; and 11:1–44). When a text that is significant in John also appeared in Mark (as, for example, the stories of the anointing woman and the women at the cross and empty tomb), I will simply note the difference between the way in which the two evangelists relate the story. Before drawing conclusions about the depiction of women in John, I will summarize Jesus' teachings that allude to women's experience, drawing heavily on the section entitled "John and Women's Experience," in Gail R. O'Day's commentary on John in *The Women's Bible Commentary* (Louisville: Westminster/ John Knox, 1992).

The first individuated woman encountered in John is Mary the mother of Jesus (2:1–11) in the story of the wedding feast at Cana. It is not surprising to find a woman in the context of providing foodstuffs for a feast. Palestinian weddings were elaborate parties that lasted for as long as a week, to which the guests brought provisions. To run out of food or drink would have been a serious embarrassment for the new couple, one likely to be long remembered by them and their guests. When the wine gives out, Mary, as Jesus' mother, has every right to ask him to provide more. As a guest, he was obliged to bring a present.

Leaving aside the heavy symbolism of "the hour" for John's Gospel, we note that Jesus' response to Mary in v. 4 is, on the face of it, not unlike his treatment of her in Mark's Gospel. Although it is unclear whether or not "woman" (*gynai*) was a term of respect (like "madam"), it seems evident that Jesus initially ignores his mother's request. Nevertheless, Mary instructs the servants to fill the stone jars used for purification with water and to take them to Jesus. John gives no direct indication of Jesus' effecting the miracle. He simply reports that when the liquid in the jars was taken to the steward of the feast, it proved to be excellent wine, in quantity (probably between 120 and 150 gallons).

John does not focus on the miracle, but assumes the reader knows that the Word through whom all things came to be (1:3) could effect such a change. A great deal of symbolism is attached to the wine and its quantity and superiority, as there is to the nuptial imagery (see, e.g., 3:25–30). For our purposes, however, we should note that the view of the relationship between Mary and Jesus here is consistent with that in the earlier three Gospels. There are noncanonical stories in which

Jesus uses his divine power to aid family and friends, but they do not appear in the New Testament except here where Mary attempts to intervene in Jesus' activities and is rebuffed. In 2:4, a verse some scholars take to be a Johannine insertion into an earlier tradition, Jesus dissociates himself from biological connections. The point is that Mary's role as physical mother had no role in the ministry of Jesus. Her role comes because of her faithfulness, her belief that Jesus *could* rectify the situation, which is evidenced by her instructions to the servants (v. 5) despite Jesus' apparent reluctance. She leaves the choice of whether or not to act to Jesus. In her injunction "do whatever he tells you" (v. 5), Mary invites people to do the will of God.

This story is paradigmatically important for John's gospel. It introduces the themes of "the third day" (v. 1), "the hour" (v. 5, in John a reference to Jesus' passion), and the superabundance that belongs to life in Jesus, in addition to the structural device of the "signs" (v. 11) around which chapters 1–12 (and perhaps all) of the Gospel are structured. All this happens with a woman as a catalyst for the action. In John's Gospel, Jesus' public ministry begins not with his teaching and healing but with his receiving hospitality at a wedding and returning the favor. As is frequently the case in John, the point of the story is christological: Jesus' freedom from human control, but his choice to act on behalf of humans.

Mary's presence at the Cana miracle raises the whole issue of her role in John's Gospel. She plays a larger part in John than in Mark, although she appears only twice, here and at the foot of the cross with the Beloved. Marian theology is outside the scope of our discussion. However, it is noteworthy that Jesus' public ministry begins and ends with Mary in attendance, and both scenes (2:1–11 and 19:25–27) have been subject to extensive symbolic interpretation. In both scenes Mary is described as "mother of Jesus" (2:1; 19:25–27) and is called "woman" by Jesus (2:4; 19:26). In chapter 2, when Jesus' "hour" has not come (2:4), Mary is seen as the church, a woman who brings people to Jesus. In chapter 19, when his "hour" is upon him, she represents the connection between past (Judaism/Mary) and future (Christian Community/Beloved Disciple); the former is placed in the care of the latter. Both stories point out that Jesus is in the process of creating a new view of family based not on biological connection, but on response to God as manifested in himself and his teachings. John places Mary "in the family" in both senses (as does Luke in Luke-Acts). (For more information on Mary in John, see R. E. Brown et al., eds., *Mary in the New*

Testament (Philadelphia: Fortress, 1978); R. F. Collins, "Mary in the Fourth Gospel: A Decade of Johannine Studies," *Louvain Studies* 3 (1970): 99–142; J. A. Grassi, "The Role of Jesus' Mother in John's Gospel: A Reappraisal," *CBQ* 48 [1986]: 67–80.)

In John the ministry of Jesus begins and ends in the company of women. Within that inclusion, women also exemplify the response to Jesus that the evangelist is seeking to engender. In this regard the story of the Samaritan woman in chapter 4 is particularly well known. Like the story of the "widow's mite" in Mark, familiarity with the standard approach to the pericope can limit our understanding of what it may be suggesting.

The usual reading of John 4:1–42 goes something like this. On a journey between Judea and Galilee, Jesus stops at midday at a well in Samaria that was associated with Jacob. (Recall that Samaritans were descended from intermarriage of Jews from the Northern Kingdom with their Assyrian conquerors. They held as scripture only the Pentateuch and had worshiped in their own temple on Mt. Gerizim until it was destroyed by Jews under John Hyrcanus in the second century B.C.) There he encounters a Samaritan woman who has come to draw water in the heat of the day because, it is assumed, she would be unwelcome at the well at the usual times of drawing water (morning and evening). Jesus surprises her by asking for a drink. Jewish men did not speak to women in public. Jews viewed Samaritans with distaste, and in fact the rabbis especially shunned Samaritan women, whom they viewed as perpetually unclean, menstruants from the cradle (see *Mishna Niddah* 4:1). Jesus breaks both a cultural and an ethnic taboo and a religious prohibition and begins a discussion about "living water," during which he asks about her "husband" and remarks that she has had "five husbands, and the one you have now is not your husband" (vv. 16–19). (Thus the view that the Samaritan woman is of questionable morals.) As the discussion progresses, the woman asks astute theological questions and responds intelligently to Jesus (v. 20, 25). For the first time in the Gospel, to her Jesus both reveals his messiahship and uses the "I am" self-designation that characterizes John's Christology (vv. 25–26). The woman returns to her village, shares what she knows of Jesus, and leads many Samaritans to believe in him— thus in effect fulfilling the role of the first apostle/evangelist.

The Samaritan woman is, in fact, one of the most theologically informed persons in the Fourth Gospel. She knows the regulations about ritual purity (v. 9), ancestral traditions of Israel (v. 12), the neces-

sity to worship at a valid temple (vv. 19–20), and the expectation of a
Messiah (v. 25). She is, in short, conversant in Samaritan theology
(which is not surprising since, unlike Jews, Samaritans educated religiously both male and female children), and Jesus takes her as seriously as a discussion partner as he did Nicodemus in the preceding
chapter. But is she really a woman of loose morals? If she were, when
she returned to her village to share her new-found knowledge of Jesus,
would she have received a hearing? Would the Samaritans have taken
seriously the witness of a strumpet?

One problem, of course, is that John does not tell us why the woman
came to draw water at noon. Commentators have assumed on the basis
of the exchange in vv. 16–19 that it was because she was deliberately
avoiding the company of other women who shunned her. But we don't
know that. (I should hate to have my morals impugned because I occasionally go to the grocery store late in the evening!) L. P. Prestt reminds
us that the conversation between the woman and Jesus would have
been carried out in Aramaic, not Greek ("The Samaritan Woman," *The
Bible Today* 30 [1992]: 367–71). The word for "husband" in Greek is
anēr, which the Septuagint uses twelve times to translate the Aramaic
word for "husband" or "owner," *ba'al* (see, e.g., Gen. 20:3; Exod. 21:22;
Deut. 22:22; 24:4). What did Jesus mean by asking the woman about
her *ba'als?*

It has been noted that 2 Kgs. 17:24–41, with its description of the
worship of native deities, forms part of the background of John 4.
Couldn't Jesus be speaking with her about this and not about her relationships with men? "You have been owned by five false gods, and the
one you have now is not your real owner," might be closer to what
Jesus meant. (Josephus's writings suggest that in religious discourse
the number five was a symbolic representation of Samaritans.) This
view was once widespread among commentators on the passage, but
more recent scholars have noted the disjuncture between v. 18 and
vv. 19–20. Jesus is talking about "husbands"; the woman responds by
talking about places of worship. But her comment is not disjointed or
inappropriate if the subject of the discussion is false gods.

R. G. Maccini has pointed out that the conclusions of the Jewish
rabbis did not necessarily apply to women in Samaria and that in the
Samaritan context there was no reason why a woman could not serve
as a witness since in the Pentateuch there are no *de jure* exclusions of
women as witnesses (see "Reassessment of the Woman at the Well in
John 4 in Light of the Samaritan Context," *JSNT* 53 [1994]: 35–46). But

could an *immoral* woman serve as a credible witness? When the Samaritan woman goes back to the village, she gets a hearing. This is more likely if she is known as a religious seeker or as religiously educated, than if she is of loose morals. More than one scholar has pointed out that the failure to recall that the original conversation was in Aramaic, not Greek, has resulted in the Samaritan woman's "bad reputation." Perhaps it is time to restore it. (And, even if the *baʿal* in question is a human husband, cultural circumstances could have led a woman to have five husbands without sexual immorality on her part. Perhaps she has been trapped by levirate marriage, like Tamar in Genesis 38. Perhaps she has been divorced for trivial reasons by several husbands. As we noted, husbands could divorce their wives for minor offenses. Remarriage was the one sure "social security" for women at the time, and this woman may have felt it imperative to remarry precisely to *preserve* her reputation.)

In any case, it is very clear that in John's Gospel the Samaritan woman in chapter 4 climaxes a series of conversations in chapters 2, 3, and 4 that move from disbelief to partial belief to full belief. The "Jews" (religious authorities who opposed Jesus) in 2:18–20 are skeptical of Jesus; Nicodemus in chapter 3 does not fully understand him; but the Samaritan woman comes to understand that he is the Messiah, and she serves a real missionary function in sharing her knowledge. John says the Samaritan villagers believe "because of the woman's testimony" (v. 39 NRSV; literally, "because of her word" [*episteusan . . . dia ton logon*]), exactly the same expression Jesus uses in 17:20 when he prays for his disciples, "I ask . . . on behalf of those who will believe in me through their word [*tōn pisteuontōn dia tou logou autōn*]." Moreover, John 4:38 is one of the most important uses of *apostellein* in the Gospel; it is missionary language used in the context of a woman who has been sent to sow so that the disciples can harvest. Just as the male disciples in the Synoptics left nets, boats, and counting houses to follow Jesus, this woman leaves her water jar to return to her village and to share the good news of the Messiah. She is the prototype of apostolic activity. Just as John's Gospel begins and ends with Mary in her role as faithful disciple, it begins and ends with a woman in apostolic activity, the Samaritan woman in chapter 4 and Mary Magdalene in chapter 20. But that is to skip ahead.

One of the most interesting and enigmatic gospel stories dealing with Jesus and women is frequently inserted in John at 7:53–8:11, although it is sometimes placed after 7:36, 7:44, or 21:25. Many ancient manuscripts of John omit the story of the woman caught in adultery as not belonging to this Gospel. Some scholars think it has more in common with Luke's Gospel, but most agree that it is authentic Jesus material. Since it usually appears in John, we shall discuss it here. In the story, a woman "caught in the very act of committing adultery" (8:4) is brought to Jesus by scribes and Pharisees who "said this to test him, so that they might have some charge to bring against him" (8:6). The woman's accusers have no real interest in law or justice. If they had, wouldn't they have also produced the *man* involved, since the scribes and Pharisees *say* she was caught during intercourse? (The word for adultery in v. 3, *moicheuein*, is used in the Septuagint exclusively of adultery of married persons.) They have already tried and sentenced her, and not necessarily according to law; whereas Lev. 20:10 and Deut. 22:22 prescribe the death penalty for adultery, neither mentions stoning. They hope to entrap Jesus, but he refuses to engage them. When they press their case, Jesus responds with the famous retort "let anyone among you who is without sin be the first to throw a stone at her" (v. 7).

In his commentary on this text in *Homily 33* on the Gospel of John, Augustine has set up a polarity with the woman as a sinful wretch and Jesus as the example of mercy. "Sin meets mercy," the headline might read. But this reading of the text dehumanizes and makes of the woman an object, much as the scribes and Pharisees did of her in vv. 3-5, and it ignores what is the central scene of the pericope, Jesus' relation to the religious establishment and his challenge to the status quo. In his reading of the text, Calvin worried that Jesus would be seen as abolishing legal punishments. Both interpretations overlook the fact that Jesus treats the woman as he treats the scribes and Pharisees. He behaves exactly the same way toward both, and by so doing shifts the balance of power in favor of the accused (compare v. 6b with v. 8; v. 7b with v. 10a; v. 7c with v. 11b). When he is ready, and in his own way, Jesus invites both the scribes and Pharisees and the woman they say they caught in adultery to give up an old way of life for a new way.

Why has the canonical status of this story, which scholars concur is authentic Jesus material, been so uncertain? Gail O'Day argues that it is because of the androcentric fears that it evokes ("John 7:53–8:11, A Study in Misreading," *JBL* 111 [1992]: 631–40). Jesus refuses to punish an adulteress. Did the early Christian community fear that the story would lead wives to think they could commit adultery with impunity?

Or was the motive even darker? Was the concern what would happen if female sexuality passed out of male control?

The canonical questions aside, in the story in John we see Jesus refusing to allow a woman to be objectified, to be used as an object in a masculine plot. He responds compassionately to her ghastly situation, treating her exactly as he does her accusers, inviting both to a more perfect life. "Go your way, and from now on do not sin again" (8:11). Part of the essence of Jesus' identity in John is as the one who forgives sin. This pericope illustrates his statement in 8:15, "I judge no one."

Chapter 11 of John is usually referred to as the raising of Lazarus, although most of it deals with Jesus' conversations with others, and it is generally understood to be the climactic sign of the first half of the Gospel, the prefiguring of Jesus' own resurrection. The story is dramatically framed by vv. 7–16, which indicate that Jesus' return to Judea to help his friends is literally an example of the shepherd laying down his life for his sheep (10:11). The story begins with the introduction of Mary and Martha. Bethany is described as "their village," not Lazarus's; the sisters are apparently more prominent than their brother. Although the event has not yet occurred, Mary is designated the "one who anointed the Lord with perfume and wiped his feet with her hair" (v. 2), perhaps because Mary is associated by John's community with this event or perhaps to make it clear that this is not Mary of Magdala, who was apparently also well known in the Johannine community. These two sisters send Jesus a message about their brother's illness (v. 3) that is couched in language reminiscent of that of his mother Mary in 2:3.

The characterization of Mary and Martha here is consistent with that in Luke 10:38–42. While Mary waits at home, Martha goes out to meet Jesus, and their conversation is the core of the story. It would be helpful if we could hear Martha's tone of voice in v. 21. Is her statement one of fact or of chiding Jesus for allowing Lazarus to die? Like the woman at the well, Martha's religious knowledge is evident but incomplete. When she affirms belief in the resurrection, Jesus responds with another "I am": "I am the resurrection and the life" (v. 25), which elicits the most fully developed confession in John. Martha says, "Yes, Lord, I believe that you are the Messiah, the Son of God, the one coming into the world" (v. 27). Martha's confession in John parallels Peter's in the Synoptic Gospels, and she seems to understand what she has said much more clearly that Peter did. At the outset of John's gospel Jesus' messiahship is revealed to a woman of Samaria, and at the close it is most fully confessed by a woman friend, Martha. When her sister, Mary, appears, it is as in Luke 10:39 and John 12:3 to fall at the feet of Jesus. In response to the confession of Martha and the emotional appeal of Mary, Jesus calls for Lazarus from the dead (compare John 5:25–29).

One of the great crises that early Christians faced was how to deal with the death of believers (see, e.g., 1 Thess. 4:13–18 and 1 Corinthians 15). In John 11 Mary and Martha are representative of those in John's community who had to face the challenge of the death of fellow believers. Martha meets that challenge by a full confession of faith in Jesus *before* his resurrection, and thus serves as a model for others in the community who will find themselves in similar circumstances. In John's gospel Peter plays a secondary role to the Beloved Disciple, and so it is consistent that Martha and not he would be the Johannine model of steadfast faith. Martha and Mary are those who are willing to trust in the face of death itself the new life that Jesus promises.

Mary reappears almost immediately in 12:1–11, John's version of the anointing of Jesus. Again, as in Luke 10, Martha serves. The simple phrase is deceptive because the verb "served" (*diēkonei*) comes from the same root as "deacon." It indicates that Martha has entered fully into discipleship by confession and active service (compare Mark 1:30–32 mentioned above). But it is also suggestive, since by the time John's Gospel was written, there was apparently as we noted in chapter 3, in some Christian communities an office of "deacon." Deacons, whose job it was to serve at table, were ordained by the apostles by the laying on of hands (see Acts 6:1–6, which describes serving at table [*diakonein trapezais*], using this same verb). Was Martha known to John's community as an ordained deacon?

This footwashing scene is not unlike Mark's. Here the woman is not anonymous, but Mary, the sister of a man Jesus has raised from the dead. Her extravagant hospitality is appropriate for one who "loves much," and the extraordinary gesture of letting down her hair in public does not seem to offend or repel Jesus, nor does her touch. John introduces Judas into the scene as the one who voices objection to Mary's behavior. This serves to remind the reader, who already knows the outline of the Jesus story, of the next supper scene in the gospel, where Jesus washes feet and Judas betrays Jesus.

As the narrative unfolds in John, Mary's anointing does two things for Jesus. First, it gives him the idea for the footwashing that follows in chapter 13; Mary's act becomes the means he uses to illustrate dramatically the meaning of discipleship. Second, because it is an anointing "for the day of my burial" (v. 7), it helps Jesus to understand that his "hour has come," which, incidentally, he announces publicly later in the chapter (12:20–36). It is Mary's action as much as the Greeks' coming to him that makes it clear to Jesus that the end is upon him. John adds an interesting detail to the story in noting that Mary also wipes off (*exemaxen*) the ointment with her hair (v. 3). C. H. Giblin has noted that this introduces a double prediction into Mary's action. She predicts not only Jesus' passion but his rising incorrupt. At the raising of Lazarus, it was understood that there would be a stench of decomposition (11:39). Here in chapter 12 the aroma is of perfume, but it does not need to remain on Jesus' body because he is incorruptible (see "Mary's Anointing for Jesus' Burial," *Biblica* 73 [1992]: 560–64). When Mary anoints the feet of Jesus, she not only predicts his death and incorrupt resurrection; she becomes a disciple in a technical sense as she fulfills the Lord's command in 13:14–15. Mary assumes her right to approach Jesus and express her love, and when a male (Judas) objects, Jesus not only confirms her freedom to do so but rebukes the man who would restrict her. In John, Mary and Martha are crucial characters. Martha is depicted as the representative of faith and full christological confession. Mary by her initiative represents the active practice of discipleship.

As in Mark's Gospel, the woman disciples are depicted in John as faithful to the end. They appear at the cross in 19:25–27, where they stand close by (not "afar off" as in Mark) and where, as noted earlier, Mary the mother of Jesus fulfills an important symbolic function. Although John does not directly say so, they apparently would have seen Joseph of Arimathea and Nicodemus take the body of the crucified Jesus and secure it with spices in the garden tomb. It is in their depiction of women as witnesses to the resurrection, then, that Mark's and John's gospel accounts differ significantly.

In John's first resurrection appearance (20:1–18), there are three scenes. At some risk to herself, Mary Magdalene comes to the tomb before daylight to discover the stone rolled away (vv. 1–2). She runs to tell Peter and the Beloved; they come to the tomb, assess the situation, and leave. Verse 9 makes it unclear whether they understand what has happened: they do not see the risen Lord and proclaim nothing of what they have seen (vv. 3–10). Mary, who has returned with them to the tomb (and who is apparently totally ignored by the men), weeps nearby. To her is given a vision of angels, and then an experience of the risen Lord himself. Jesus speaks to her and gives her the commission to go and declare what she has seen and the message he has for the brethren. Unlike Mark's silent women, "she told them that he had said these things to her" (vv. 11–18).

In John's Gospel, people bear witness to what they have seen and heard (compare 1 John 1:1–3). Thus, Mary's credentials as witness to the resurrection are impeccable. There can be no question but that Mary Magdalene has the honor of primacy in apostolic witnesses; she is, as is so often noted and so infrequently understood, "the apostle to the apostles." (She certainly meets the Pauline qualifications for the title "apostle.") John apparently regards a woman as the primary witness to and guarantor of the pascal mystery. Mary's story is a harsh one. She has seen her much-loved Jesus die in ignominy and agony. She has faced the possibility that after this indignity, his tomb has been desecrated. When she seeks to share this information with Jesus' male disciples, she has been ignored. She waits and weeps, and her persistence is rewarded.

When asked by the angels why she weeps, she responds that "they have taken" not "the Lord" but the more personal "my Lord" (v. 13). When asked by "the gardener" what she seeks, (*zētein*, a verb connoting diligent search), Mary assumes that this stranger may know where Jesus' body is, and she assumes the initiative to retrieve it. Although there is consolation for her when she recognizes Jesus, the central theological issue in Mary's meeting is not personal. It echoes the first view we have of Jesus in John 2, where Jesus declines to be controlled by human, here female, expectations. Commentators who make much of the fact that Jesus will not allow the female Mary to touch him (v.17) but invites the male Thomas to do so (20: 27) miss the main point of the story. The risen Lord entrusts the news of the resurrection and its effect to a woman. A bereaved woman is important enough to Jesus that he interrupts his journey to God to speak with her and to give her words to speak: "go to my brethren (*adelphous*) and say to them, 'I am ascending to my Father and your Father, to my God and your God'" (v. 17). The message echoes the text of Ruth 1:16, and it is the first time Jesus calls believers "brothers and sisters." At the footwashing scene he calls them no longer disciples but friends (15:13–15). Now, after the resurrection, they are siblings. The death and resurrection of Jesus have brought him and his followers into the same family with the same parent. The blood and water from the side of Jesus have brought forth the new family that was prefigured in his life and teaching and at the foot of the cross. That Christians are siblings is one of the fundamental teachings of the New Testament. It is a teaching that was first entrusted to a woman. It is, in fact on the "testimony" (a great Johannine theme) of a woman that the whole Christian faith depends.

So far as I have been able to discern, there is only one woman who is depicted negatively in John, and she is neither named nor a follower of Jesus. In chapter 9 Jesus heals a man born blind. To ascertain the veracity of his healing, the Pharisees call in "the parents of the man who had received his sight"(9:18). The plural would indicate that both father and mother were summoned. The parents affirm that the healed man is their son, but with regard to his healing refuse to say anything, "Ask him; he is of age. He will speak for himself" (9:21). The parents are afraid of being excluded from the synagogue (9:22), a reality faced both by the healed man (9:34–35) and by John's community. Apparently in this story, under pressure from religious authorities, a woman abandons her son under official inquiry. One might wish for more maternal loyalty, but John's Gospel depicts reality. Women and men sometimes act ignobly under pressure from those who have power over them.

Finally, then, when it comes to the teachings of Jesus as John records them, nothing is said which addresses or influences women directly. John's Jesus, unlike the Jesus of the synoptics, does not tell parables (so women are not depicted as characters in parables), nor is there the ethical material in John that appears in the Synoptics (for example, teaching on marriage or divorce). However, the discourse material in John does have implications for women's experience. The best exposition of this occurs in Gail R. O'Day's commentary, which I summarize in what follows. (For a lovely, short exposition of how women are models of God's redemptive encounter with humans, see Jane Kopas, "Jesus and Women: John's Gospel," *Theology Today* 41 [1984]: 201–5.)

First, O' Day points out that in John's Gospel love and mutuality are ethical categories. Loving relationships are to categorize the Christian community (13:35), not patterns of dominance and submission. Nor is self-denial ("cross bearing," as it is sometimes termed in a misreading of Jesus' words in the Synoptics) the mark of a Christian, an important point for women who have often been socialized to deny the self rather than to develop and share its giftedness. Mutuality is encouraged by the vine metaphor in John 15. According to John's Jesus, individuals in the Christian community are members of an organic unit. They are branches joined to a common vine. In contrast to the radical individualism of the West, mutuality is valued. This should lead to nonhierarchical structures, since no "branch" has special status; each is held in life by its connection to the vine. In John's Gospel, love and mutuality, not dominance and individualism, are virtues disciples should embody.

Second, O' Day reflects on the "Father God" language in John. God is called Father more frequently in John's Gospel than in any other New Testament book. As I pointed out in the introduction to this book, language is important. What are women to make of a Gospel that refers to God in exclusively masculine terms? O'Day points out (as have several feminist scholars writing on Christology, most notably Elizabeth Johnson in *She Who Is* [New York: Crossroad, 1992]), that the Father God language in John is essentially relational and not patriarchal. That is, Jesus calls God Father and refers to God as the Father of those who believe in language that is intended to express the intimacy of family life. As was pointed out in the discussion of John 20:1–18, becoming "children of God" (1:12–13), sharing with Jesus his divine parentage, is one of the great gifts of discipleship. Family language characterizes the Gospel. While the "father language" may be off-putting to some feminists, it should not be set aside or "neutered" by paraphrases, but understood as fundamental to Johannine theology, which intends to describe the intimate relationship with God which becomes possible through Jesus.

The overall picture of women in John, then, as it is in Mark's Gospel, is very positive. Women are depicted as independent followers of Jesus. Only two women, Mary the mother of Jesus and Mary the wife of Clopas, are introduced in relationship to men. John's women played unconventional roles of which Jesus appears to have approved, sometimes overruling the men who objected. John's Gospel begins and ends with the Mother of Jesus as an exemplary disciple and with women in the role of evangelist/apostle. As Raymond Brown noted, discipleship is the primary Johannine category, and John's Gospel presents women as "first-class" disciples. Women and men were commissioned as agents of the word and stood at the foot of the cross as representatives of Jesus' true family. It is not irresponsible to draw the conclusion that in the community of John the evangelist, women and men must have exhibited a considerable degree of equality in the life of discipleship.

BIBLIOGRAPHY

Brown, R. E. "Women in the Fourth Gospel." *Theological Studies* 36 (1975): 688–99.

Fletcher, M. E. C. "The Role of Women in the Book of John." *Evangelical Journal* 12 (1994): 41–48.

Kopas, J. "Jesus and Women: John's Gospel." *Theology Today* 41 (1984): 201–5.

O'Day, G. R. "John." In *The Women's Bible Commentary*, edited by C. Newsom and S. Ringe, 293–304. Louisville: Westminster/John Knox, 1992.

Schneiders, S. M. "Women in the Fourth Gospel and the Role of Women in the Contemporary Church." *Biblical Theology Bulletin* 12 (1982): 35–45.

Thiessan, K. H. "Jesus and Women in the Gospel of John." *Direction* 19 (1990): 56–64.

CONCLUSIONS

The Gospels of Mark and John present a universally more positive view of women than do the letters of Paul. That is, whereas Paul seems to be ambiguous in his discussions of and about women, the evangelists' depictions of women in their narratives and their reports of Jesus' words show women in a positive light. It is hard to conclude that the Gospels of Mark and John are only patriarchal texts. The history of their interpretation may well have been. But the material *in* those Gospels describes autonomous women who respond to Jesus and to the Gospel and who are affirmed for doing so both by Jesus in the narrative and by the evangelists in their preservation of the traditions. This suggests that the communities from which the Gospels of Mark and John come must have been communities with strong women who may have held positions of leadership. The material on women and Jesus in these Gospels would reflect not only traditions about Jesus known to the evangelist and his community, but traditions reflective of the community itself.

This presents us with an interesting historical problem, one we shall speak of in more detail in the chapter on Deutero-Pauline materials. It is a commonplace of feminist commentary on the New Testament that at the earliest stages Christianity was more egalitarian than it was later in its history. So we aren't surprised to find Mark, written about 70 A.D. reflecting that early equality. But what about John? John was written at the very end of the first century, probably at about the same time and in the same geographical provenance as some of the earliest Deutero-Pauline works (Ephesians, for example). In the later Pauline works we begin to see limitations placed on the activity of women. The interesting problem, for which I have no satisfactory answer at this point, is why John retains the earlier position vis-à-vis women at the same time that his contemporaries are beginning to restrict their activity within the Christian community. While it is undoubtedly true to say that John is preserving original Jesus material, that answer seems a little too simple.

In any case, the overall picture we have of women in the Gospels of Mark and John suggests some interesting trajectories for Christology as well as for ecclesiology. First, when we think of Jesus as one who proclaimed justice and liberation (as per Isa. 61:1–3) that message must include women. Jesus' characteristic behavior of including, affirming, accepting women as equals is part of his larger inclusion of and preference for the marginalized. This is supported by his calling women to be disciples with men, and this was undoubtedly part of his offense in the eyes of the religious establishment.

Second, when we recall the "Father God" language of John, it must be understood as part of the dismantling of patriarchy. Elizabeth Johnson has pointed out that "Father" (*Abba*) is the opposite of a dominating patriarch (*Consider Jesus* [New York: Crossroad, 1992]). On the contrary, to call God *Abba* is to be drawn into the new family that Jesus attempts to create, into a new community of mutuality whose members are brothers and sisters. To call God Father is, on one level, to subvert patriarchy by affirming the filial mutuality of the kingdom of God (see Matt. 23:9–12).

The Father God of the parable of the prodigal son in Luke 15:11–32 is, as Sandra Schneiders pointed out, "the one who respects our freedom, mourns our alienation, waits patiently for our return, and accepts our love as pure gift" (*Women and The Word* [New York: Paulist, 1986], 47). It is not, therefore, Jesus' maleness that images this God, but his inclusive love, his acting in Godlike ways. The Jesus who affirms a Syrophoenician woman reflects the God who protected and provided for Hagar. The Jesus who criticizes a religious system that would demand of a widow her financial security reflects the God of whom the prophets speak in their criticisms of corrupt religious practice (see, for example, the book of Amos). The Jesus who allows the extravagant love of the anointing woman reflects the God of Hosea and of the Song of Songs and who rejoices when the one whom the soul seeks is found. The Jesus who first appears to women and commissions them to proclaim his resurrection is the God who knows and appreciates that "love is strong as death" (Song 8:6).

Jesus was a man who undercut the values of the patriarchy of his day. Had he been a woman, there would have been nothing revelatory about his actions. Women were expected to nurture and to serve. Jesus' denunciation of injustice was so potent because it came, as it were, from within the ranks of the oppressors and brought "good news to the oppressed" and proclaimed "liberty to the captives" (Isa. 61:1).

BIBLIOGRAPHY

Brennan, I. "Women in the Gospels." *New Blackfriars* 52 (1971): 291–99.

Chilton, B. "The Gospel of Jesus and the Ministry of Women." *Modern Churchman* 22 (1978–79): 18–21.

Harris, X. J. "Ministering Women in the Gospels." *The Bible Today* 29 (1991): 109–12.

Kee, H. C. "The Changing Role of Women in the Early Christian World." *Theology Today* 49 (1992): 225–38.

Morrison, M. "Jesus and Women." *Sojourners* 9 (1980): 11–12, 14.

5

The Lukan Texts: Luke and Acts

INTRODUCTION

THE TITLE OF THIS VOLUME is *Women in the New Testament: Questions and Commentary*. It is intended to suggest that the work is a presentation of part of the discussion in a lively and ongoing conversation, not a final delivery of answers. The works attributed to Luke, the Gospel of Luke and the Acts of the Apostles, provide a case in point of the questions.

For many years the Lukan texts dealing with women were understood to be stalwart allies of Christian feminism and feminist interpretations of the New Testament. One of the early commentaries of this century, Charles R. Erdman's *The Gospel of Luke: An Exposition* (Philadelphia: Westminster, 1922), called Luke the "gospel of women" and noted how many stories with women as primary characters Luke alone records. The stories of Mary and Elizabeth, Anna, the widow of Nain, and Mary and Martha were touted as examples of Jesus' inclusiveness and Luke's community's equality with regard to women disciples.

More recent feminist scholarship, especially that done in the 1980s has been more skeptical about whether Luke is indeed unqualifiedly pro-woman. For example, it has now been noted that Luke's is the one Gospel in which "wives" are included among those who can be left behind for the gospel (14:25–26). The women in the Gospel who most fully receive Jesus' unqualified approval are the penitent (7:36–50) and Mary (10:38–40), neither of whom speaks at all. Luke omits altogether the story of the Syrophoenician woman, who "bests" Jesus in debate (see Mark 7:24–30 and Matt. 15:21–28). And the story of Mary and Martha, in fact, pits woman against woman.

So the question that is raised is whether or not Luke-Acts is really favorable to women. The discussion of the texts that follow, especially those from the Gospel of Luke, provide an opportunity for us to experience the wide range of feminist scholarship and to puzzle over this aspect of the New Testament's presentation of women.

BACKGROUNDS

Luke-Acts is a two-part work intended to be read in sequence. Luke presents the good news of Jesus, the gospel, and Acts presents the good news of the church, what people did in response to that gospel. In Luke Jesus moves from Galilee to Jerusalem, toward the center of the Jewish world. In Acts the "Way" of Jesus moves from Jerusalem to Rome, the center of the Greco-Roman world. The last chapter of Luke is directly tied to the first chapter of Acts; each contains appearances of the risen Jesus, proofs of his existence, his commission to his disciples, and his ascension.

The two books are roughly parallel. Each has a prologue (Luke 1:1–4; Acts 1:1–5), followed by the coming of the Spirit (Luke 1:5–2:52; Acts 1:6–2:47). In Luke there is a baptism, a temptation, and a Galilean/Palestinian ministry (3:1–7:60); in Acts a baptism and a Jerusalem/Judean/Palestinian ministry (3:1–9:50). Jesus travels from Galilee to Jerusalem (Luke 9:51–10:44), and the church travels from Jerusalem to Rome (8:1–28:16). Jesus has a Jerusalem ministry that ends in his martyrdom (Luke 19:45–24:53), and Paul has a Roman ministry which, presumably, ended in his martyrdom (Acts 28:17–31). This parallelism suggests that Luke outlined the two works so that the materials would agree and echo each other. (And there are, as well, many thematic similarities as the ministry of the church in Acts mimics the ministry of Jesus as it is presented in Luke.)

Luke's Gospel comes from the middle period of Gospel writing; it was written after Mark (on which it depends) and before John. Three concerns seem to dominate the Gospel. First, Luke may well be the first New Testament writer to understand that the parousia, the return of Christ in glory, might be delayed. Much has been made of his view of salvation history. In his work *Die Mitte der Zeit* (English *The Theology of St. Luke* [New York: Harper, 1961]), Hans Conzelmann argued that Luke thought in historical terms of a remote and an immediate past and an immediate and a distant future. All history is from the hand of God. Luke's distant past was the era of the Law and the Prophets, in which God was preparing a way for redemption by giving the Law and Prophets (see Luke 16:16). Luke's immediate past was the era of Jesus, the time of the proclamation of the kingdom of God and the center of history, a time when God broke down the exclusivism of Judaism and included Gentiles, women, Samaritans, and other "untouchables." It was a time when prophecy was fulfilled (see Luke 4:14–30). The future, which stretched forward from Pentecost to the parousia, was to be the time of the proclamation of the gospel by the church with Jesus as the paradigm for action. Apparently God delayed the parousia to allow the church to spread the gospel message.

A second Lukan concern was the destruction of the Temple in Jerusalem. Most scholars believe that the Temple had been destroyed by the time Luke wrote (see Luke 21:20). Some think that, in Luke's view, the destruction of Jerusalem was the consequence of Jesus' passion there. Thus, Rome becomes the new center of gravity for Christians, and, as the political center of the world, it was the ideal place from which to spread the Christian message.

Third, Luke is concerned about the relationship between Christians and the Empire. With Jerusalem destroyed and Christians being expelled from the synagogues, the church was in a tenuous position. If Jesus were to return immediately, it could revile the Empire and await *its* destruction. If, however, the parousia were delayed, Christians must not only live in the Empire but come to terms with it. Luke writes with a conciliatory view of Rome. In various ways Luke depicts the Romans as sympathetic toward Christianity. (For example, in Acts the Romans intervene several times to help the apostle Paul.) Paradoxically, Luke wants to depict Christianity as the fulfillment of, and having transcended, Judaism, but to claim the status of *religio licita* (a legal religion) by virtue of association with it.

Luke, in short, writes with an eye toward influencing Rome positively toward Christianity. (And, as we shall see, this influences his portrayal of women.) The primary audience for Luke's writing is Gentile or Roman. For these people a literary approach that would not jar educated tastes was required. And so, using the Septuagint as his stylistic model, Luke writes in the mode of a Roman historian, using literary forms and conceits drawn from that world. In short, Luke is a classic apologist. To Romans who would have viewed Christianity as having sordid origins (it sprang from the suspect Jews), Luke demonstrates Christianity's universality. To Romans who would mistrust Christianity as "upstart" or "newfangled" Luke presents Christianity as the fulfillment of God's ancient plans and purposes. To those who thought Christianity politically dangerous (Nero attacked Christianity, and Claudius expelled the Jews from Rome because of a riot over one "Chrespus," probably "Christus"), Luke depicts the Empire as the great protector of the new movement.

Dedicated to a Gentile, the Theophilus of Luke's prologue (1:1–4; compare Acts 1:1–5.), the Gospel commends Christianity to a Gentile world; Luke argues that church and state can live peaceably together. His writings were not only an apology to the Empire but a tool for its evangelization. Christianity is commended in terms the Greco-Roman world found palatable. And within the Christian community, Luke-Acts served to document one view of the spread of Christianity and of its great Gentile missionary, Paul, and to defend against the nascent Gnostic heresy that invaded the community when it moved into the Gentile world.

Who was this clever and literarily gifted apologist? The earliest traditions about the writer come from the Muratorian Canon, which was collected in Rome about 170 A.D. It records "the third book of the gospel, according to Luke, Luke that physician . . . after the ascension of Christ, when Paul had taken him as companion of his journey, composed in his own name on the basis of report." It continues by noting that Luke was a Syrian from Antioch, a doctor by profession, and an associate of Paul until the apostle's martyrdom, who remained unmarried and died in Boeotia at the age of eighty-four.

That Luke makes no claim to eyewitness status regarding the life of Jesus is admitted in the prologue of the Gospel, but the "we" passages, which begin in Acts 16, have traditionally been taken as his "travel journal." There are three brief references to "Luke" in the New Testament. Philemon mentions a Luke as Paul's fellow worker, and 2 Tim. 4:11 notes that a Luke was alone in staying with Paul in the days of his imprisonment. Finally Col. 4:10–14 mention a Luke, a physician and Gentile. Are these references to Luke the evangelist? It is unclear. It is true that men taken to Rome as prisoners were allowed two slaves. Paul was from Tarsus, which had a renowned medical school. Physicians in the Hellenistic world often began as slaves. Did Paul meet Luke there and take him as a personal servant to Rome? But if Luke were a companion of Paul, why does Acts reflect no knowledge of

Paul's epistles and little understanding of the apostle's main theological concerns?

The only thing that can be said with certainty is that Luke was a Gentile Christian. He was probably writing after 70 A.D. but before the end of the century. No ancient tradition suggests a place of composition, but the works were long associated with various cities in Greece. Luke's view of Judaism, his literary conventions, and his vocabulary make it probable that he wrote outside Palestine in a Christian community with strong Gentile and female membership. Because traditions in the Gospel are often redacted to reflect well-to-do persons and circumstances, and because the Gospel has a special concern for the poor and oppressed, it is suggested that its community was one that had both very wealthy and seriously marginalized members. Parables like the rich fool (Luke 12:13–21) and the rich man and Lazarus (Luke 16:19–31, told only by Luke) suggest that Luke's community had rich members who needed to be reminded about their obligations to the poor in their midst. This concern for affluence further supports an urban origin for the Lukan writings.

Luke's special concern for the poor and the outcast is a general manifestation of his concern for women and their place in the Christian community, and it is to that issue we now turn.

WOMEN IN THE GOSPEL OF LUKE

We have already noted that Luke has both many women characters and many passages dealing with women. Nearly one-third of the material unique to Luke deals with women. After chapters 1 and 2, which, as the accounts of Elizabeth's and Mary's pregnancies, are "women's stories" (the word "womb" occurs seven times in these two chapters: 1:15, 31, 41, 42, 44; 2:21, 23), there are fifteen texts in Luke with significant women characters and no fewer than nineteen passages in which women or the traditional work of women is focal. It has been noted by numerous scholars that one of Luke's compositional characteristics is to pair stories about men and women. In his Anchor Bible Commentary, Joseph A. Fitzmyer calls this "step parallelism" (*The Gospel According to Luke* [New York: Doubleday, 1981], vol. 1). So, for example, we have annunciations to Zechariah and to Mary in chapter 1. In chapter 7 Jesus cures the centurion's dying son and raises the widow of Nain's son from the dead. In chapter 18 two illustrative parables pair a persistent widow and a humble tax collector. Other examples are numerous and easily located. Turid Seim has noted that in this gender pairing order seems unimportant. While Luke depicts a world divided by gender, he does not apparently give one gender literary precedence over the other.

An overview of the women in Luke reveals that they appear in miracle stories (Simon's mother-in-law [4:38–39], the widow of Nain [7:11–17], the daughter of the synagogue ruler [8:40–42, 49–56], the hemorrhaging woman [8:42–48], the crippled woman [13:10–17]), as followers of Jesus (8:1–2; 23:49), and in the "man-woman parallel" kingdom parables (13:12–21; 15:4–10; 18:1–14). Widows are especially prominent in Luke and usually appear in a positive, exemplary light (Anna [2:36–38], the widow of Zarephath [4:25–27], the widow of Nain [7:11–17], the persistent widow [18:1–8], the victims of "hypocrites" [20:47], and the generous widow [21:1–4]). The widows are a case in point of Luke's mixed economic community, and it might well be that Luke highlights widows positively because the Christian communities he knew were slow to admit them for fear they would be a financial burden. (We shall have reason to mention this again in our discussion of the Pastoral Epistles in chapter 6.)

Luke's Hellenistic heritage may help to account for the large number of women found in his Gospel. I pointed out in chapter 1 of this work that Greek women enjoyed more legal freedoms than Palestinian Jewish women and that, relatively speaking, Roman women had the greatest degree of legal and social emancipation. Luke's Gospel was probably shaped in a community that was influenced by Roman law, one in which there were probably numerous women in leadership positions within the church and numerous women to be catechized.

Luke apparently had a special interest in women. But if one compares Luke's depictions of women with his depictions of men, as Jane Schaberg does in her article on Luke's Gospel in *The Women's Bible Commentary*, Luke's attitude toward women becomes a bit clearer. There are ten named women in Luke's Gospel and thirty-nine named men (not including the seventy-six in the genealogy). There are ten unnamed women in the Gospel and forty individual men. In Jesus' teaching in Luke women are mentioned 18 times, men 158 times. Women speak fifteen times in Luke, and in only ten instances are their words given. Schaberg thinks a simple comparison of this nature betrays Luke's androcentric bias.

Several of the stories in Luke in which women are prominent also appeared in Mark, although they have been redacted by Luke to serve his purposes (Simon's mother-in-law, the anointing woman, Jairus's daughter, the hemorrhaging woman, the generous widow at the Temple, the women at the crucifixion and the empty tomb). Rather than review that material again, in what follows I shall provide brief commentary on texts that are exclusive to Luke and shall pay special attention to Luke 8:1–3 and 10:38–42 as illustrative of the "mixed reception" these texts are now receiving among feminists. Then, as was the pattern established in the chapter on Mark and John, I shall turn to the ways in which women and women's concerns appear in the Lukan didactic material, the teachings of Jesus.

The first two chapters of Luke stand alone for several reasons. They provide a unique view of the birth story of Jesus. Characters are introduced who appear in no other Gospel. These chapters are unique in their introduction of hymns into narrative Gospel material. The fact that they read very differently from the rest of the Gospel narrative (one can skip from 1:4 to 3:1 and find the transition quite smooth) has suggested to some scholars that they may be skillful translations into Greek from an original Hebrew document. It has been suggested that Luke had access to this material and, finding nothing in it offensive to Romans, translated it and appended it to his Gospel. Certainly the material in chapters 1 and 2 most closely resembles the Septuagint and seems to be based on the story of Hannah in 1 Sam. 1:1–2:11.

After a literary prologue (1:1–4) dedicating his work to Theophilus and explaining his methods and goals, Luke turns to the infancy of Jesus. That story is structured around seven scenes, each of which is laid out in two pairs of stories. The basic pattern is that of the annunciations (to Zechariah [1:5–25] and to Mary [1:26–38]), united by a visit of the two mothers (1:39–56) and that of the births (of John the Baptist [1:57–80] and of Jesus [2:1–21]). Beginning with a focus on female characters, with women in the leading roles, the narrative suggests at the outset God's reversal of the world's values. Luke opens what for him is history's most important story, that of Jesus, with the least important people in his society, a barren wife (Elizabeth), a virgin peasant girl (Mary), and a widow (Anna).

The gospel begins with Zechariah and Elizabeth, stressing: "*Both* of them were righteous before God, living blamelessly according to all the commandments and regulations of the Lord" (1:6 [italics mine]). God rewards their faithfulness by allowing Elizabeth, who was previously barren, to conceive. Likewise, Mary "a virgin engaged to a man whose name was Joseph" (1:27; Joseph himself does not appear in the story until chapter 2), is "favored" by God and cooperates with God's plan for salvation. The gift of the Holy Spirit (who was of particular concern to Luke and is, in fact, a focal "character" in Acts) comes first to Elizabeth and Mary, whose faithfulness sets the tone for the rest of the Gospel. Each behaves rightly in her religious context. Elizabeth, Mary, and Anna prefigure the women in the rest of Luke. Although marginalized by the rest of society, these faithful women are God's instruments in salvation history.

That Joseph takes his betrothed to Bethlehem to participate in the Roman census is a clear signal to Luke's Roman readers that the central figures in Christianity had no quarrel with Roman rule (2:1–5). And Joseph and Mary keep the rites of their own religious tradition, circumcising their child on the eighth day and following the purification rites of the law of Moses. This latter they did by visiting the Temple in Jerusalem, where another man-woman pair is encountered, Simeon, a devout and spirit-filled man (2:25–35), and Anna, a widow and prophet (2:36–38), each of whom praises the child Jesus and predicts great and terrible things for him—although no words of Anna are recorded, and Simeon is given a hymn.

The infancy narrative in Luke closes with the story of the boy Jesus in the Temple. His devout parents "went to Jerusalem for the festival of the Passover . . . as usual" (2:41–42). We see prefigured in the account of Jesus remaining behind to converse with the teachers not only the conflict between Jesus and official Judaism but the conflict between obedience to God and family responsibility that will characterize much of Luke's presentation of discipleship. When Mary (not Joseph) asks Jesus about his behavior, he makes the distinction between the earthly and heavenly family, and Mary responds with absolute silence: she "treasured all these things in her heart" (2:51).

The opening chapters of Luke focus on the traditional women's role of bearing children. The women we meet here are the only women given speeches, and the only ones not subsequently corrected by men. Elizabeth functions as a prophet when "filled with the Holy Spirit" (1:41); she blesses Mary and the fruit of her womb (1:42), and she utters the only christological confession by a woman in the Gospel when she speaks of the "mother of my Lord" (1:43). Mary is the only woman in the Gospel to be given a speech of proclamation (1:46–55). She is Luke's ideal female believer, totally submissive to God and, from chapter 2 on, a model listener. The widow Anna (2:36–38) is called a "prophet," but she never utters a word. The emphasis is on her long widowhood and piety. In short, Luke opens his gospel with three potent female characters and then seems to back away from such strong characterization of women. These three are notable for fulfilling socially acceptable roles and for silent, obedient piety. They present a "mixed message" about women, who are depicted both as major players and as conventional female role models.

After Simon's mother-in-law (4:38–39), who appeared also in Mark, the next female character in Luke's gospel is the widow of Nain (7:11–17). As Jesus approaches the town of Nain, he encounters a funeral procession; "a man who had died was being carried out. He was his mother's only son, and she was a widow" (7:12). The point is that this woman is not only bereaved at the loss of a child, but, without a husband, she has no male advocate and essentially, therefore, no legal identity. The son's loss is a double burden for the widow, and the large crowd attending the funeral is evidence of the sympathy for her position. When Jesus raises the man from the dead, he is not only restoring a son to his widowed mother but is restoring a woman to her place in the accepted social order.

Instead of foreshadowing resurrection at the end of the Jesus' public ministry as John does in the raising of Lazarus in chapter 11 of his gospel, Luke places this image of resurrection near the beginning of Jesus' work. The widow of Nain is both an individual woman for whom Jesus has compassion and a silent representative of all who have been deprived of personal worth, of all who have been defined in terms of social relationship to men (as wives or mothers). Note that what Jesus does for her is to return her to the social order. He restores her to her role as mother. Certainly this is a compassionate gesture, one that speaks to her emotional and potential economic distress, but one might ask if it is ultimately liberating?

In Luke, Mark's anointing woman (14:3–9) becomes "a sinner" (7:36–50). Rather than prefiguring the burial of Jesus and serving as prophet and priest, Luke's woman becomes the occasion for a parable about forgiveness and love. She does not speak at all, and she, along with the silent Mary in 10:38–42, most fully receives Jesus' approval. It is she who is improperly linked with Mary Magdalene (who is not mentioned in this text) by means of the Mary named in John 12:1–3. Although completely inaccurate, this conflation of characters dominates the popular imagination (see J. Schaberg, "How Mary Magdalene

Became a Whore," *Bible Review* 8 [1992]: 30–37, 51–52). In Luke the prophetic and political dimension that is strong in Mark's and in John's accounts of the scene is subsumed in the emotional response of the woman to Jesus. While this outcast takes on herself the servant role of discipleship, it is notable that Luke omits Mark's remark that "what she has done will be told in remembrance of her" (Mark 14:9).

One wonders if the story of the anointing woman precedes 8:1–3 to exemplify the sort of woman who traveled with Jesus and the Twelve through Galilee. In any case, the text (one long sentence in Greek that is divided into two sentences in most English translations) is one of the most interesting and important Lukan records about women. First, it demonstrates that women traveled with Jesus and the Twelve. Second, it gives the only indication in scripture of the source of financial support for Jesus' mission. The text appears in the midst of a series of stories dealing with women (the two texts we have just discussed, the mother and brothers of Jesus [8:19–21], and the dual healing of the synagogue ruler's daughter and the woman with a hemorrhage [8:40–56]). It points forward to the passion narrative, where the same women reappear (23:49; compare Matt. 27:55–56 and Mark 15:40–41).

There is no synoptic parallel to this account. In literary composition, it is distinctively Lukan with its parallelism and exacting detail. All of Luke's major themes are in evidence here: the universalization of the gospel, the qualities of true discipleship, the good news to the poor and marginalized. In short, the text accurately reflects Luke's understanding of Jesus' mission. But what does it reflect about the evangelist's view of women?

On the face of it, these women are highly liberated. They have apparently left home and family to travel with Jesus, *with* his approval. This suggests, as Ben Witherington has noted, that Jesus intended from the beginning for women to be witnesses of and participants in his mission ("On the Road with Mary Magdalene, Joanna, Susanna, and other Disciples," *ZNW* 70 [1979]: 243–48). Some of these women have been healed or exorcised of demons by Jesus. Mary of Magdala was delivered from seven demons. Joanna, wife of Chuza, Herod's steward, was a highly placed woman. A steward had charge of the household and estates of his master. So Joanna represents the high-born women, who also appear prominently as converts to Christianity in Acts. Susanna is a Hebrew name. So the named women here illustrate the breaking down of social distinctions that characterized the ministry of

Jesus and the early Christian movement. (Or do they represent the fact that women can work together without need for cultural or socio-economic distinctions among themselves?)

The response of these women to their deliverance is to follow Jesus, the standard response of discipleship, and to provide for Jesus and/or his disciples (there is a textual variant in v. 3) "out of their resources" (*hyparchontōn*), from what was at their own disposal. Women of some means traveled with Jesus and the Twelve (thus receiving the teaching the men received) and "served" Jesus, a primary function of discipleship.

And herein is an interesting puzzle. The Greek word for "provided for," *diēkonoun* (v. 3), has as its root *diakoneō* ("to serve," "to wait on," "to serve *as a deacon*"). It is related to *diakonos* ("helper," "servant," "minister," "deacon"). We noted concerning Paul's writings and Mark and John that by the time of the writing of the Gospels there was apparently a function called "deacon" in the early Christian community which involved both serving at table and perhaps some undefined liturgical function (see Acts 6:1–6). The standard reading of Luke 8:1–3 has been that the women mentioned therein exercised the traditional female role of hospitality in the service of Jesus and the disciples. But to be a "deacon" in this sense was to fulfill a specific role in the Christian community. And as R. J. Karris has noted, 75 percent of the usages of *diakonein* in Luke mean not "serving tables" but serving as "go between," "herald," or "messenger," that is, as proclaimer of the word of Jesus ("Women and Discipleship in Luke," *CBQ* 56 [1994]: 1–20; see also J. N. Collins, *Diakonia: Reinterpreting the Ancient Sources* [New York: Oxford University Press, 1990]). Karris believes that the women in Luke 8:1-3 used their resources in going on a mission for Jesus.

Luke certainly means to depict the women as exhibiting a proper response to Jesus, following and serving, but does he also mean to suggest that Jesus understood women as his witnesses and messengers? If so, the text moves us far beyond the traditional female role of hospitality. Although Luke never explicitly calls women disciples, the women here are described *as if* they were disciples. Furthermore, "with him," *syn autō* (v. 1) is a technical term for discipleship elsewhere in Luke (see 8:38; 9:18; 22:56). In Luke's Gospel, following Jesus, being his disciple, means detachment from possessions, family, and personal plans. Don't Mary Magdalene, Joanna, Susanna, and the other women exemplify these qualities?

On the other hand, Jane Schaberg has noted that these women are described in the nonreciprocated role of service to the males. She wonders if the women really traveled freely with Jesus or made day trips from home bases. (My suggestion in this regard is that in Galilee Joanna, at least, was relatively far from home if her husband was looking after Herod's estates in Judea.) Does Luke think of women as a separate group within the larger group of Jesus' followers, a group dedicated to domestic service? In Shaberg's view, the traditional reading of Luke 8:1-3, that some women traveled with Jesus and his disciples and provided for them from independent sources of wealth, does not square with the understanding that most of Jesus' earliest followers were poor. Is this text primarily about powerful women who accompanied Jesus and served as his witnesses, or is it another object lesson on wealth and the right use of possessions, an important Lukan theme? (see 12:15–21; 16:19–31; 19:1–10).

My own view is that Luke 8:1–3 is a powerful description of the ministry of women in the community of Jesus. It grants them a status close to that of the Twelve and describes them in semitechnical terms. The Christology of Luke's gospel, which depicts a serving Lord Jesus, in fact gives increased dignity to the roles of service undertaken by the women. But, within the community of women scholars, my view is but one of several. This same divergence in interpretation is evident in the other distinctively Lukan text devoted to women characters, Luke 10:38-42, the story of Mary and Martha.

The text occurs relatively early in what scholars refer to as Luke's "longer insertion" (9:51–18:14), a section of the Gospel framed as a journey and used for the presentation of episodic teachings of Jesus that come largely from Q (the sayings source shared by Matthew and Luke) and L (Luke's own, distinctive sources of information about Jesus). The sense of travel is communicated by frequent reference to movement (9:51, 57; 10:38; 13:22; 17:11) but not by geographical references, which suggests that Luke was unfamiliar with Palestinian geography. Crowds travel with Jesus, so these teachings are directed to them as well as to his own disciples. Often the teachings occur in the context of a feast or meal, frequently one including the Pharisees. Luke's Jesus is seen with a variety of people, some wealthy, some poor, some religious officials, some "sinners."

The account of Martha and Mary occurs after a trip through Samaria (9:51–62), the sending out and return of the seventy (some of whom were probably women, since Luke 24:6-7 assumes that the women at the tomb remember teachings offered here and elsewhere to the

Galilean disciples), and the teaching on eternal life, which culminates with the parable of the Good Samaritan (10:25–37). Some scholars have suggested that 10:38–42 is the "woman half" of another Lukan pairing of stories that demonstrate the nature of love, for neighbor in 10:25–37 and for Jesus/God in 10:38–52. It is certainly a story about the values of the kingdom of heaven, but what values? Who is being valued and for what?

In the popular reading of this text, Jesus comes to the home of Mary and Martha and finds Martha distracted by overwhelming domestic duties. Martha hopes Jesus will command Mary to help her. Instead, Jesus affirms Mary's desire to study with him and, in effect, includes Mary in the rabbinic circle. This reading has led to several interpretations. First, the sisters are viewed as representative of theological principles. Martha represents justification by works; Mary, justification by faith. Or, in Augustine's view, Martha represents this world and Mary the next. Or, in Origen's view, Martha represents action and Mary contemplation. Thus, many Roman Catholic readings of the text suggest that the two sisters represent two life-styles: Martha is the laywoman and Mary the religious or nun. Some have seen the passage as placing liturgical ministry over diaconal, and many have seen it as the justification of theological education for women.

But Elisabeth Schüssler Fiorenza has pointed out that the traditional readings are all androcentric. They pit woman against woman and Christian women against traditional women's roles in Judaism. Martha and Mary begin as equals, but then Martha asks Jesus to scold Mary, which places the women in a relationship of dependency on a male authority figure. In fact, many women identify with Martha and resent the fact that Jesus takes Mary's side in the dispute. And the outspoken woman in the story, Martha, who speaks up for herself, is silenced in favor of the subordinate Mary (see "A Feminist Critical Interpretation for Liberation: Mary and Martha, Luke 10:38–42," *Religion and Intellectual Life* 3 [1986]: 21–35). Even the way we refer to the story, as the story of *Mary* and Martha, subtly diminishes Martha.

What is really going on in the pericope? First, recall that it occurs in the travel narrative in Luke and follows the sending out of the seventy. When Jesus enters "a certain village" and is received by Martha (note that the text says the house belongs to her, making Martha one of several well-to-do, independent patronesses in Luke-Acts), the reader is expected to recall aspects of the mission of the seventy (10:5, 7, 8, 10), including "being received" (10:8, 10). To be received (v. 38, from *dechomai*) means both to be given hospitality and to have the mission one represents accepted. Martha embodies a positive response to the mission of Jesus. That Mary is Martha's "sister" [that is, both biological sister and fellow believer, as per Paul's usage of the term *adelphos*) includes her in this positive response.

Martha, we are told in v. 40, "was distracted by her many tasks," literally "by much *serving*." Again, the Greek word is *diakonian*, which in Luke is used more in the context of "activity of an in-between kind," "spokesperson," than of "waiting tables." *Diakonia* in Luke-Acts, as was pointed out above, denotes participation with others in leadership and ministry on behalf of the community. Six of its eight uses in Acts point to leadership in the church and proclamation of the gospel. Is Martha's "serving" domestic activity or ministry? It may well be that Martha is distracted by "much ministry." Jesus does not criticize the form of Martha's ministry so much as the anxiety and agitation she feels in it.

If this is the case, then Martha's difficulty with Mary is a perception that her sister (biological and/or fellow Christian worker) isn't "pulling her weight" in the work of ministry. As W Carter points out, the story may be told by Luke to help his readers understand ministry as an act of partnership ("Getting Martha Out of the Kitchen," *CBQ* 58 [1996]: 164–280). It is not enough to *hear* the word of God; one must *do* it. Mary's listening is good, but she must do. A textual variant on v. 39 reads "Mary who *also* sat at the Lord's feet" (*he kai* and suggests that both sisters were among Jesus' students. Martha's doing is good, but she must remember to listen. Martha is being distracted from ministry's source (Jesus himself) by too much doing. Mary Rose D'Angelo more or less concurs with Carter's reading. She understands Martha and Mary to be one of a series of pairs of women ministers in the New Testament ("Women Partners in the New Testament," *JFSR* 6 [1990]: 65–86). The two women, she thinks, headed a house-church and *both* were students of Jesus' teachings.

Schüssler Fiorenza, however, offers an entirely different, and not nearly so positive, view of Martha and Mary. She agrees that the *diakonian* of Martha is a technical term for ecclesial leadership in the church that met in her house. As John 11 makes clear, Mary and Martha were well-known figures in the early church. Martha has a clearly christological faith. Here in Luke she calls Jesus "Lord"; in John she makes a full christological confession (see John 11:27). Mary shows the proper practice of discipleship, but in the Lukan story the women are pitted against each other. Jesus is appealed to and the result is a word that restricts women's ministry and silences women like Martha who led house-churches. In short, Schüssler Fiorenza thinks that this story in Luke reinforces the societal and ecclesiastical polarization of women (like that which is found in the Pastoral Epistles). It limits a woman's role to that of listening to Christian instruction (given by men).

In the history of biblical scholarship there are many examples of reputable scholars holding widely divergent views about the same text. Luke 10:38–42 is a case in point of the same phenomenon in feminist biblical scholarship, and this fact may mark the coming of age of our scholarship. Scholars of the Gospels agree that the stories told about Martha and Mary (and all the material in the Gospels) are at the service of their author's larger theological purposes. The question with regard to Luke can be framed as follows: Is his purpose to include the excluded (here, women), to demonstrate the universality of the Christian mission, or to limit the roles of women in the church in order to harmonize its practice with general movement of society in the Empire after the promulgation of the Augustinian marriage laws?

Lukan scholars, particularly those trained in feminist methodology, read 10:38–42 both ways. But most concur on two points. First, and in agreement with traditional readings of the passage, the story of Martha and Mary is evidence that at an early stage of the development of the Jesus movement women were active as leaders in it. They were full participants in ministry and in study. Second, Luke 10:38–42 is not a text that pits domestic service against study or traditional women's roles against a more "liberated" activity; it does not describe a conflict between housework and headwork. There is no reference in the text to a meal. The textual variant in v. 42 (rendered "few things" or "little" is necessary [P38, P3] or "few things are necessary or only one" [Nestle text] or "one thing is necessary" [oldest papyri and *koine* group]) has been incorrectly understood as a comment on Martha's unnecessarily elaborate meal preparation. That Luke chooses a term that has strongly technical associations in his writing to describe Martha's work in v. 40 (*diakonian*) should disabuse future interpreters of this mistaken reading.

If the story of Martha and Mary were intended by Luke to limit women to passive roles in the church, it has been used contrary to Luke's intent. Rather than undermining women's participation in the active ministry of the church, Luke 10:38-42 has been used to argue in favor of their preparation for it, an irony that should not be lost on either interpreters who read the text as liberating for woman or those who see it as placing limitations on women.

The other narrative text focussing on a woman that is found only in Luke is 13:10–17. This text describes the miraculous cure of a crippled woman that is the occasion for a controversy with the leader of a synagogue. The woman has been crippled for eighteen years. "She was bent over and was quite unable to stand up straight" (13:11), apparently afflicted with osteoporosis. Unafraid to touch a woman whom he apparently does not know (he cannot know whether or not she is "unclean"), Jesus restores her by laying hands on her. The synagogue leader is offended because the healing occurs on the Sabbath. Jesus castigates him and the assembly because they are more concerned for their livestock than for another human being. "Does not each of you on the Sabbath untie his ox or his donkey from the manger and lead it away to give it water? And ought not this woman, a daughter of Abraham whom Satan bound for eighteen long years, be set free from this bondage on the Sabbath day?" (vv. 15–16). The text is another in which Luke's Jesus reaches out to the unfortunate and to women. Jesus not only heals the woman's physical infirmity; he acknowledges her value in the religious community by explicitly calling her a "daughter of Abraham," a designation found only in Luke.

The remaining women in the Lukan narrative also appear in the Synoptic parallels. The generous widow in Luke 21:1–3 appears in the same context as she does in Mark, and the Lukan text may be read much as the Markan (see the previous chapter on Mark and John). But Luke's depiction of the women in his passion and resurrection narratives (chapters 22–24) is somewhat different from either Mark's or John's.

First, more than one scholar has noted that there is strong evidence in Luke's Gospel that a group larger than the Twelve male apostles were present at the Last Supper (Luke 22:1–38). The most extensive presentation of this view is Quentin Quesnell's article "The Women at Luke's Supper," in *Political Issues in Luke Acts* (Maryknoll, N.Y.: Orbis Books, 1983). After establishing the fact that women were part of the larger group around Jesus as he entered Jerusalem and taught in the Temple, Quesnell points out that nothing in the content of the teaching at the Last Supper indicates that it was addressed only to the Twelve, and some statements are, in fact, inconsistent with being only to them. Nothing in the text or context of 22:14 suggests that the

Twelve were alone with Jesus. In fact, there are several textual variants with regard to "the apostles" in 22:14. In P75.B, the first hand of Codex Sinaiticus and Codex Bezae Cantabrigiensis the reading is "apostles," but the corrector of Sinaiticus changed "apostles" to "Twelve" presumably to strengthen this Gospel's ties with Mark and Matthew. "The Twelve apostles" was combined in Codex Ephraemi, Alexandrinus, and the Western Text and became the *kcine* reading, which tended to render attendance at the supper more narrowly. Interestingly, at 22:14 Sinaitic Syriac reads *mathētai autou,* the most inclusive rendering, "his disciples." The NRSV translation has, appropriately I think, returned to the earliest reading of v. 14, simply "apostles," a much more ambiguous term than "the Twelve."

Nor does the context limit attendance at the Last Supper to the Twelve. For example, Luke 22:26 notes, "the greatest among you must become like the youngest, and the leader like the one who serves," presuming both older and younger persons in attendance and our recollection that women were listed among those "who served" in the Gospel. In fact, for good or ill, the only persons in Luke who are said to "serve" are women (see 4:39; 8:3; 10:40). Furthermore, 22:28 would include others who persevere with Jesus ("you are those who have stood by me in my trials") among the dinner guests. Luke alone does not specify the number of thrones from which the followers will judge. In 22:30 the twelve tribes will be judged, but there is no mention of twelve thrones for the judges.

Perhaps the most persuasive argument for the inclusion of women at the Last Supper in Luke is the evangelist's insistence that the Last Supper was the Passover: "Now the festival of Unleavened Bread, which is called the Passover, was near" (22:1). "Then came the day of Unleavened Bread, on which the Passover lamb had to be sacrificed" (22:7). "So they went and found everything as he had told them; and they prepared the Passover meal" (22:13). Passover was normally eaten in the family with women and children present. Both had parts to play in the Passover liturgy. Therefore, Joachim Jeremias expressed surprise at absence of women at the Lord's Supper, as well he might! (*The Eucharistic Words of Jesus* [New York: Macmillan, 1955]).

Several details of Luke's presentation of women after the crucifixion suggest their presence at the Last Supper. Most strikingly, 23:55–56 reports, "The women who had come from Galilee followed, and they saw the tomb and how his body was laid. Then they returned, and prepared spices and ointments." These same women go to the tomb early the first day of the week, find it empty, and receive a message from two men in dazzling clothes, "and returning from the tomb, they told all this to the eleven and to all the rest" (24:9). All thirty Lukan uses of the verb *hypostrephō* ("return") indicate a going back to the place from which one had earlier departed. It seems clear enough that the women returned to the eleven and "the rest" who were in the upper room, the location of the Last Supper, the place they knew and returned to because they had previously been there.

Although the evidence is not conclusive, it is tantalizing and not unreasonable to surmise that, in Luke's view, women were present at the Last Supper. They are certainly clearly in evidence throughout his passion narrative. Luke's is the only passion narrative that includes the lament of the women of Jerusalem (23:27–31). Certainly their lament is for an innocent rabbi unjustly tried and condemned, but is it also for a man who has treated them with unusual attentiveness and inclusivity? In any case, Jesus' response to them is consistent with his teaching elsewhere in the gospel. If an innocent man meets such a fate, what will be the fate of the guilty?

At the foot of the cross are "all his acquaintances, including the women who had followed him from Galilee" (23:49). "Followed" (*synakoloutheō*) was a technical term for discipleship in 5:11. Both 23:49 and 55 ("the women who had come with him from Galilee followed") recall 8:1–3. It seems to me that Luke is establishing the women from Galilee as reliable witnesses to the resurrection of Jesus. In 24:1–12 these same women from Galilee are on center stage. They discover the empty tomb, receive the word from "two men in dazzling clothes" (v. 4), and are asked to remember the words of Jesus given as teaching *to his disciples* in Galilee (vv. 6–8). Notably, in Luke the women are not charged to "go and tell," and when Mary Magdalene, Joanna, Mary the mother of James, and the other women with them report to "the eleven and *the rest*" (italics mine; does "the rest" include other women?), "these words seemed to them an idle tale, and they did not believe them" (v. 11). To the apostles, the witness of the women is no more than the babbling of the fevered or delirious, although the Emmaus travelers quote the women's testimony along with that of other Jerusalem believers (24:22–24) and report their experience of the risen Jesus to "the eleven *and their companions* gathered together" (24:33 [italics mine]). It is to this same group (which, as Acts 1:14 clearly attests, included women) that Jesus appears in 24:36–49, displays his crucified and risen body, and eats broiled fish; and it is to

them that the risen Lord declares, "you are witnesses of these things"
(24:48).

The narrative of Luke's Gospel begins and ends with women in
prominent roles, and it contains several accounts apparently known
only to Luke, in which women are focal. Interpreters vary widely in
how they "read" these passages vis-à-vis women. Before any conclusions can be draw about "women in Luke," however, the didactic and
"sayings" material must be reviewed.

Even a cursory reading of the discourse material in Luke reveals a
striking number of references to women and women's spheres of activity. Luke's Jesus evinces wide knowledge of domestic life and
"women's work." By my reading Jesus refers to women's work nineteen times in the Gospel. He refers to the image of a house swept and
kept in order, clearly woman's work (11:25). He is knowledgeable
about baking (see references to yeast in 12:1; 13:21) and grinding meal
(17:35). There are several striking maternal images in Jesus' teaching.
He describes the human condition as the condition of those "born of
woman" (7:28). He compares himself to a mother hen who gathers her
chicks under her wings (13:34) and is especially sympathetic toward
the plight of pregnant women and nursing mothers in times of tribu-
lation (21:23).

The texts from Hebrew scripture that Jesus chooses for preaching
and illustration often include women. Perhaps the most significant
allusion in his sermon at the synagogue in Nazareth is to the widows
at the time of Elijah (4:25–26). And in 17:28 he enjoins his hearers to
"remember Lot's wife." Jesus' interpretation of the laws concerning
and his own pronouncements about marriage and divorce inevitably
favor or improve the status of women. Jesus' teaching on divorce in
16:18 discourages putting away one's wife for trivial reasons. The man
who does so and marries another woman commits adultery. As in the
parallel texts in Mark and Matthew, when Jesus is asked about levirate
marriage (20:27–40), he refuses to assume that the woman is a posses-
sion to be passed among brothers and instead speaks for God's higher
view of marriage and raises the level of discussion to that of the nature
of resurrection life. And, as we have noted, Jesus was particularly concerned for widows. He implicitly commends the widow who stands up
for her rights in the parable of the widow and the unjust judge (18:1–8),
and he criticizes the scribes who "devour widows' houses" (20:47).

Interestingly, in a time when one's biological family was critical in
social and religious life, Jesus seems to set it aside in favor of the cre-

ation of a new notion of family based on allegiance to him and to his teachings. When a woman listening to his teaching cries out, "Blessed is the womb that bore you and the breasts that nursed you" (11:27), that is, "blessed is your biological mother," Jesus responds, "blessed rather are those who hear the word of God and obey it" (11:28). Jesus realizes that his teaching will cause division in families (12:49–53). He tells the crowds following him, "Whoever comes to me and does not hate father and mother, wife and children, brothers and sisters, yes, and even life itself, cannot be my disciple" (14:26). And it is only in Luke's Gospel that wives are included in what must be left behind for the sake of the kingdom of God (18:29–30). Biological family is to be replaced by the family of believers; and, in Jesus' day and culture, that clearly placed a special burden on women and wives, who were dependent on family structure for livelihood.

In analyzing the place of women in the Gospel of Luke it may be helpful to ask a preliminary question. Was Luke primarily a historian or a theologian? If we understand Luke to be a historian, then it is easier to read the stories in his Gospel as pro-woman. On the surface at least, they depict women as prominent in Jesus' life, ministry, and teaching. If, on the other hand, we view Luke primarily as a theologian and look at the material in his Gospel redactionally (in comparison with the other Gospel writers, to discern what editorial changes and additions Luke has made), the evangelist's presentation of women is not nearly so easily categorized. The roles in which women appear are likely to be ones acceptable in imperial society. While Luke multiplies stories about women, indicating that numbers of women must have been part of his community, those stories depict women in entirely predictable and usually silent activity. But before we can draw any final conclusions about Luke's view of women in the church, we must take into account the second of his two contributions to the New Testament, the Acts of the Apostles.

BIBLIOGRAPHY

Carter, W. "Getting Martha Out of the Kitchen, Luke 10:38–42." *CBQ* 58 (1996): 264–80.

Karris, R. "Poor and Rich: The Lukan *Sitz im Leben*." In *Perspectives on Luke-Acts*, edited by C. Talbert, 112–25. Darville, Va. Association of Baptist Professors of Religion, 1978.

_____. "Women and Discipleship in Luke." *CBQ* 56 (1994): 1–20.

Kopas, J. "Jesus and Women: Luke's Gospel." *Theology Today* 43 (1986): 192–202.

Maly, E. "Women and the Gospel of Luke." *Biblical Theology Bulletin* 10 (1980): 99–104.

Quesnell, Q. "The Women at Luke's Supper." In *Political Issues in Luke-Acts*, edited by R. Cassidy and P. Sharper, 59–79. Maryknoll, N.Y.: Orbis Books, 1983.

Ryan, R. "The Women from Galilee and Discipleship in Luke." *Biblical Theology Bulletin* 15 (1985): 56–59.

Schaberg, J. "How Mary Magdalene Became a Whore." *Bible Review* 8 (1992): 30–37, 51–52.

———. "Luke." In *The Women's Bible Commentary*, edited by C. Newsom and S. Ringe, 275–92. Louisville: Westminster/John Knox, 1992.

Schüssler Fiorenza, E. "A Feminist Critical Interpretation for Liberation: Mary and Martha, Luke 10:38–42." *Religion and Intellectual Life* 3 (1986): 21–35.

Seim, T. K. "The Gospel of Luke." In *Searching the Scriptures*, Volume 2, edited by E. Schüssler Fiorenza. New York: Crossroad, 1994.

Via, J. "Women, the Discipleship of Service and the Early Christian Ritual Meal in the Gospel of Luke." *St. Luke's Journal of Theology* 29 (1985): 37–60.

WOMEN IN THE ACTS OF THE APOSTLES

The Acts of the Apostles is, like Luke's Gospel, addressed to Theophilus, and it opens with a reminder that it continues the story of Jesus after "he was taken up to heaven" (1:1). Acts is written as if it were a work of history, although it contains many kinds of writing, including speeches, biography, prayers, and letters. That it is not an objective account becomes evident when one compares Paul's life as recounted in Acts with his own reports in his epistles. (See Galatians, for example.) Acts is the story of the church told from Luke's theological perspective. It completes the story of what God was doing in Jesus. Luke understands the growth of the church to be a work of God accomplished by means of the empowering Holy Spirit. The message of Jesus is presented first to Jews as the fulfillment of their prophetic scriptures, and then to Greeks and others as the means of deliverance from fate and death.

Jesus' description in Acts 1:8 of the empowering descent of the Holy Spirit which will lead the disciples to be his witnesses "in Jerusalem, in all Judea and Samaria, and to the end of the earth," in fact provides the outline of the book. Acts chronicles Peter's work primarily in Jerusalem and Judea (chapters 1–7), Philip's mission to Samaria (chapters 8–12), and Paul's missionary work in the Greco-Roman world (chapters 13–28). Acts describes the movement of Christianity from Jerusalem (center of Judaism) to Rome (center of the "pagan" world), that is, from Jerusalem to the "end of the earth."

Luke the evangelist is certainly the author of this work, which was written at about the same time as the Gospel (80–90 A.D.). A more vexing question is the issue of Luke's sources. Some scholars argue that there is no tradition behind Acts like that behind the Gospels. That some sections of Acts are written in first person plural (the "we" material, which begins in Acts 16) has led others to suggest that either Luke used his own travel journal or that of another eyewitness. A few students of Christian origins think Acts' author had access to records of churches in the various cities mentioned. Although Luke's sources cannot be identified with certainty, it seems clear that he followed the formal models found in Hellenistic history and the stylistic precedents of the Septuagint.

As is the case in the Gospel, Luke's view of women as it appears in the Acts of the Apostles is complex. Although a number of women are mentioned, far fewer women than men appear. A careful reading even suggests that women are purposely excluded from centrality in Acts. Luke mentions Mary in the upper room in Acts 1:14, but the fact that the other women there are nameless suggests their secondary status. Major speeches and/or sermons in Acts are explicitly directed to men (see, e.g., 1:11, 15; 2:14, 41; 3:17; 13:6; 21:17; 22:1; 23:1; 28:17]. In circumstances of direct address Luke's characters prefer gender-exclusive terms like "brothers," "men," or "fathers." This use of masculine forms of address in public discourse is but one suggestion of a wider Lukan position, that the public world is the world of men and the domestic sphere that of women. When requirements for filling out the ranks of the Twelve are stated, one is that the person must be a man (1:21). (All the other requirements could have been met by the women from Galilee who discovered the empty tomb.) Although women appear with the apostles and disciples in Jerusalem early in Acts (1:14), no women were apparently present at the Jerusalem council in chapter 15. In Luke's Gospel women accompanied Jesus in his ministry and were faithful through his death and resurrection, but later are apparently not deemed appropriate vehicles for public proclamation. (Recall that even in Luke's resurrection accounts women are discounted as witnesses.)

However, the fact that before his conversion Saul persecuted both male and female Christians (8:3; 9:2) indicates both that women were full members of the Christian community and that they were considered by Saul as equally dangerous. Acts presents the Christian message as appealing to both men and women. About five thousand men who heard the message of Jesus through Peter and John believed (4:4). A great number of men and women who heard the message preached in the Temple accepted it (5:14). Cornelius had gathered his relatives and close friends in Caesarea, and that group which apparently included men and women responded to Peter's preaching (Acts 10). Likewise, the whole households of both Lydia and the Philippian jailer were converted by Paul (chapter 16). In Thessalonica, Paul converted "not a few of the leading women" (17:4), and likewise at Beroea many believed "including not a few Greek women and men of high standing" (17:12). In Athens, one Damaris became a Christian (17:34), and the household of Crispus in Corinth were converted (18:8). In Tyre Christians appear "with their wives and children" (NRSV 21:5. Actually, as Gail R. O'Day points out in her essay on Acts in *The Women's Bible Commentary*, the word for "wives" and "women" is the same in Greek [gynē], and nothing in the context would suggest "wives" above "women" here. We can equally well read this as a statement of the inclusiveness of Tyre's Christian community). Acts depicts both men and women as responding to the message of Jesus, although women converts seem to be more prominent in Paul's missions to Gentile cities than they were in and around Jerusalem.

Several scholars have noted that the prominence of women among the converts of Paul's Gentile mission is entirely consistent with the picture we have of religious life in the Greco-Roman world. Women were the mainstay of religion in that world. Their tendency to "dabble" in religion was, in fact, criticized by Juvenal's fourth satire. (See also the fictionalized but highly accurate treatment in Thornton Wilder's novel *The Ides of March.*) The Pastoral Epistles recognize such behavior and warn against it, as we shall see later in this study.

Acts names twelve women: Mary the mother of Jesus (1:14); Sapphira (5:1); Candace the Queen of Ethiopia (8:27); Tabitha (Dorcas, 11:36); Mary the mother of John Mark and apparently leader of a house-church (12:12); Rhoda, a servant girl (one of the few named Christian slaves in the New Testament) (12:13); Lydia, a businesswoman and leader of a house-church (16:14); Damaris, an Athenian convert (17:34); Priscilla, the wife in a missionary couple (chapter 18); Diana/Artemis, the patron goddess of Ephesus (19:23); Drusilla, wife of Felix (24:24); Bernice, wife of Agrippa (25:13, 23, 30). In addition, Acts mentions the widows in the church in Jerusalem (6:1-6), Jewish women of high standing in Pisidian Antioch (13:50), Timothy's Jewish mother (16:1), a slave girl with a spirit of divination (16:16-18), and four daughters of Philip of Caesarea who were prophets (21:9). Taken together, these women represent an astonishing number of categories including married, single, professional, "homemaker," Jew, Greek, Roman, goddess, sister, mother, mother-in-law, prophet, missionary, teacher, queen, and slave. This great diversity suggests how dangerous it is to generalize about "women in the early church." Methodologically, it is more helpful to examine carefully references to each of the various women mentioned.

I take issue with J. Jervell's article "The Daughters of Abraham: Women in Acts" (in *The Unknown Paul* [Minneapolis: Augsburg, 1984]). Jervell argues that the women in Acts did not exercise any leadership function. Of the Christian women mentioned, several apparently were leaders in their churches. Priscilla along with her husband Aquila (chapter 18) was a teacher and missionary to Syria and Ephesus. Priscilla was apparently well known among Paul's communities (see Rom. 16:3-4; 1 Cor. 16:19) and for that reason could not be excluded from mention by Luke. The daughters of Philip (21:9) were prophets, a shadowy but clearly noted "office" in the early church (see 1 Cor. 12:28-29; Eph. 4:11-12). It is, I think, noteworthy that Luke's Gospel opens with a quotation from Joel that speaks of the prophetic outpouring of the Spirit on men and women, but that when Luke mentions these prophetesses, they are silent. And the other female prophet in Acts, the Philippian slave girl with the oracular spirit (16:16-19) is silenced by Paul. (I shall return to the "problem" of women's prophetic ministry in the conclusion of this chapter.) Tabitha is called a "disciple," and she apparently took responsibility for the order of widows in her area (11:36). Both the mother of John Mark (12:12) and Lydia (16:14) at the very least allowed Christians to meet in their homes and probably led house-churches. So long as the canon of the New Testament was in flux and different groups and localities appealed to different authorities, there was a wide variety in the practice of leadership in the early church. This variety is apparent in Acts in the roles which women assumed in the Christian community.

The most recent book-length study of which I am aware on women in Acts is *Women in the Acts of the Apostles,* by Ivoni Reimer (Minneapolis: Fortress, 1995). Reimer examines in detail the most important passages in Acts that focus on women (5:1–11; 9:36–43; 16; 18:1–3, 18–19, 24–28). I am indebted to her work and use it here, although I shall survey only two representative stories, that of Tabitha (9:36–43) and that of Lydia (16:11–15, 40), which I take to be parallel. That is, Luke has provided both Peter's mission and Paul's with one pericope in which a leading woman is central. Both Tabitha and Lydia are women who serve as benefactresses to their Christian communities and thus are in leadership positions.

The story of Tabitha (Aramaic for "gazelle," thus the Greek "Dorcas" ["gazelle" or "deer"]) in 9:36–42 is another example of Lukan pairing of a story about a man with one about a woman. In 9:32–35 Peter has healed the paralytic, Aeneas, and in 9:36–42 he raises Tabitha from the dead. The peace in the church that is described in 9:31 gives Peter the opportunity to make pastoral visits. (Lydda was about two-thirds of the way between Jerusalem and its port city, Joppa, thirty-nine miles northwest.) Luke depicts him as a miracle worker in the line of Elijah (1 Kgs. 17:17–24) and Elisha (2 Kgs. 4:18–37), and his activity here mirrors that of Jesus in the Gospel (Luke 7:11–17; 8:41–42, 49–56; and John 11:1–44). In Acts missionary advances are heralded by signs and wonders. The miracles of chapter 9 prepare for the missionary advance into Gentile culture, which follows with the conversion of Cornelius's household in 10:1–11:18. Peter's raising of Tabitha from the dead is the first time an apostle of Jesus performs a miracle of this magnitude. The point is to show that the power of Jesus is available to his followers, to confirm the gospel promises by showing Christ at work in the church.

Two aspects of the story are of particular interest with regard to women. Verse 36 describes Tabitha as "a disciple." The masculine form of the word, *mathētēs,* means a disciple, pupil, or follower and is the term chosen by the evangelists to describe followers of Jesus including the Twelve. In the whole New Testament the female form, *mathētria,* is found only here in Acts. This lexicographical fact can be read in two ways. Perhaps it means simply that Tabitha was a member of the Christian religious community in Joppa.

On the other hand, there is some confusion in the Gospels about whether the term means the Twelve or a larger or smaller circle around Jesus. There is no consistency among the Gospels about the number of disciples or who they were. In an article entitled "The Twelve" (in *Women Priests*, edited by L. Swidler [New York: Paulist, 1977], 114-122), Elisabeth Schüssler Fiorenza notes the lack of consistency in naming the Twelve and points out that "twelve" is a symbolic number and may not refer to twelve individual male followers of Jesus. Mark, she notes, identifies the Twelve and disciples, pointing out that both are proven by suffering with Jesus (as the faithful women do).

Another interesting use of *mathētria* sheds some light on the issue. In the *Gospel of Peter*, an apocryphal gospel that was probably written in Syria in the mid-second century, *mathētria* is applied to Mary Magdalene. The text reads as follows: "Now early on the Lord's day Mary Magdalene, a disciple [feminine form in Greek] of the Lord, . . . took her women friends with her and came into the tomb where he was laid." In Coptic Gnostic literature *mathētria, mathētai,* and *apostoloi* (apostles) are used synonymously in a list headed by Mary Magdalene.

The most conservative reading of the Lukan use of *mathētria* in Acts 9:36 is that Tabitha was a follower of Jesus. But, in view of the other uses of the term, there is the possibility that Tabitha was closer to Jesus. Note that Peter goes immediately to her aid without any explanation from those who summon him (vv. 38–39). How did he know her? From her reputation for "good works and acts of charity" (v. 36, both frequently touted activities in the New Testament) or because she had been among the "other women" who traveled with Jesus and the Twelve and ministered to them? Residents of Joppa might well have heard of the work of Jesus in Jerusalem and become his disciples. And Tabitha is described as engaged in activity very much like that of the ministering women in Luke 8:1–3. Furthermore, the Greek text of Acts notes that there was "a *certain* [female] disciple" (v. 38) indicating that a number of women disciples lived in Joppa. Who were they? Probably the widows whom Tabitha served.

Several scholars have suggested that the widows mentioned in vv. 39 and 41 were already a special group within the church (see the regulations for this group in 1 Tim. 5:3–16). Verse 41 speaks of the "saints," which would be all the Christians, and then names the "widows," as if they were a subgroup in the larger category (as, indeed, they were in Acts 6:1–6, where they receive aid from the Jerusalem church). Since no husband is mentioned, it may well be that Tabitha herself is a widow (like Mary in 12:12, Lydia in 16:14, Phoebe in Rom. 16:1, and Chloe in 1 Cor. 1:11). Was she the leader of the congregation of widows in Joppa, and thus the foremother of the group of women which was the most prominent in the church from the late first through the third centuries? (see B. Thurston, *The Widows* [Philadelphia: Fortress, 1989]). St. Basil (ca. 330–379) interpreted Acts to mean that Tabitha was a widow in this ecclesial sense. Certainly her home seems to be the first example of a Jewish-Christian house-church outside Jerusalem.

It has been suggested, wrongly I think, that the widows in v. 39 are professional mourners. Tabitha, at any rate, was actively looking after other widows, fulfilling the spirit of 1 Tim. 5:16, "if any believing woman has relatives who are really widows, let her assist them; let the church not be burdened. . . ." The church in Joppa values her for her "almsdeeds" and "acts of charity," language reminiscent of that used about patronesses of Hellenistic synagogues. (And note that at 10:2 Cornelius is also described as devout, God-fearing, and a doer of good works.) Interestingly, Tabitha is doing the same work that men do in 6:1–6. There the work is called *diakonia*, but the technical term is not used for Tabitha. She is understood as a model of discipleship, but what she does is called good works or almsdeeds; the same activity that is performed by men and called "ministry" by Luke. Luke may not have wanted to use "leadership language" in regard to Tabitha, but she was so well known and her memory was so deeply enshrined in the Christian community that he could not omit her story from Acts.

Parallel to Tabitha in the ministry of Peter is Lydia in the ministry of Paul, and her story occurs as part of another Lukan pairing. The conversion of Lydia's household (16:11–16) is related before the conversion of the Philippian jailer's household (16:25–34). Her story forms part of the movement of the church onto European soil related in Acts 16, where in v. 11 the fascinating "we" material in Acts begins. According to Luke, Paul is engaged in his second missionary journey. Having been prevented by "the Spirit of Jesus" from entering Mysia, Paul is summoned by the vision of a Macedonian to "come over . . . and help us" (16:9), which he proceeds to do, thus taking the gospel for the first time into Europe.

In Philippi, a Roman colony with special rights and privileges, Paul finds a congregation of women at "a place of prayer" (v. 13), a *proseuchē*, a term that Reimer points out is understood in Josephus, in parallel literatures, and in inscriptions to be a synagogue. (Paul's customary missionary practice is to visit synagogues first; see 13:14; 16:13; 17:16–17.) This is the only text in the whole New Testament that presents a gathering only of women. The verb for "gathered," *synerchesthai*, is frequently used in connection with "synagogue." (In 1 Cor. 11:17–34 and 14:23–26 Paul uses it as a technical term for the coming together of Christians for the Lord's Supper.) Paul and his associates join the women and "sit"; they assume the rabbinic position for teaching. Acts 16:13–15, then, may be a source for the participation of women in synagogue worship in the Diaspora.

Among the women gathered is Lydia. Three things are notable about her. First, she is clearly a professional woman, a *porphyropōlis*, "a dealer in purple cloth" (v. 14). Her hometown, Thyatira was famous for purple dyes, which were extracted either from the veins of shellfish (thus making those dealing in it "unclean" by Jewish standards) or from the roots of the madder plant. Production of textiles was traditionally woman's work, but part of that work would have included travel to sell the cloth produced. The whole occupation was considered by the Roman upper classes "dirty work" (*sordidus* or *sordidum*). Second, Lydia is described by Luke as Cornelius was in 10:2 as a "worshiper of God," a "God-fearer," a term used to describe a Gentile who accepted the truth of the Jewish religion but who had not been circumcised. Thus, she is "theologically literate" in the Jewish tradition. When Paul preaches to her, he preaches to one who was knowledgeable.

Third, Lydia is the head of her own household, thus probably either a single woman or a widow. Because a number of people were required to produce and dye cloth, Lydia's household might have been extensive, and may thus have been a considerable community of Christians after its conversion. The house-church, which was typical of the Pauline mission, provided leadership opportunities for women because the household was considered woman's appropriate sphere of influence. Well-to-do women in the first century were known to have opened their houses to oriental cults for worship. As noted in chapter 3, Philippi was especially noted for cults with strong, central female figures. Thus, to offer hospitality to Paul and his fellow missionaries involved some risk.

Lydia is one of the few women in Luke who speak, and she uses her "speech" to offer the traditional female gift of hospitality. Lydia "prevailed upon" (*parabiazesthai*) Paul to "come to my house." The word is found outside the New Testament to describe circumstances in which a crisis or life-threatening event is avoided. In pressing Paul and his company to come to her home, Lydia is offering them protection. At the same time she is putting herself at risk for she is "aiding and abetting" a "carrier" of a cult that might be thought of as non-Roman. She is putting herself in the position of the women who supported cultic activity. She invites these itinerant men to her home with apparent disregard for her own reputation or for the effect it might have on her business.

Paul's first European congregation is made up of women. In Gentile Macedonia there were apparently not ten Jewish men to make up a synagogue congregation, but faithful women met to worship nonetheless, were receptive to Paul's preaching, and, according to Acts, became his first European converts. Lydia's home became the meeting place for these new Christians (vv. 15 and 40). One wonders if Paul's letter to the Philippians was addressed to her home. In that letter, as we saw, there was little hint of limitation on women in the Christian community. Women were so prominent and powerful that many scholars think a disagreement between two of them threatened to divide the church (Phil. 4:2). This picture of the importance of women in the Philippian church is, as we noted in chapter 3, consistent with Polycarp's letter to the Philippians (ca. 155 A.D.) and with other literary and archaeological records.

What Acts presents in Lydia is a woman who had practiced Judaism independently of men and who then responded to the gospel as preached by Paul and led her household to Jesus, subsequently giving the church she helped to found a place to meet in her home. In Philippians, Paul called women like Lydia "fellow workers" "for they have struggled beside me in the work of the gospel" (4:3). Though Luke uses no ecclesial or technical language with regard to her, at the very least Lydia is Paul's first named European convert and a symbol of his success among women in the Greek cities. Like Tabitha, she is the benefactor of a Christian community, and in the line of Lukan women who "provided for . . . out of their means."

One final view of women in Acts deserves note. At the outset of this section I suggested that the women in Acts present us with a varied picture. Most of the Christian women Luke includes in the Acts of the Apostles he describes in positive terms. But this is not the case with Sapphira, wife of Ananias, whose story is told in Acts 5:1–11. Consistent with the common property experiment carried out by the early church (2:45; 4:32–37), Ananias and Sapphira sold a piece of property.

Scholars note that Sapphira's knowledge of and approval of its sale suggests that it was part of her *kĕtûbâ*, her "prenuptial arrangement." But the couple do not give all of the proceeds of the sale to the church; they withhold a portion of it and attempt to deceive Peter about its existence. As a result God punishes them with sudden death.

Sapphira's role in this deception is active. She approves the sale and the deception, so she too is punished. "And great fear seized the whole church and all who heard of these things" (5:11). Luke clearly relates the story as a cautionary tale to warn others away from transgressing against community solidarity. But from a feminist perspective too, the pericope sounds a note of warning. Sapphira is characterized by a lack of self-determination. She goes along with her husband when she knows he is doing wrong. Her complicity leads to death.

In relating his "theologized" view of the spread of the Christian message in Acts, Luke is presented with an interesting dilemma. He clearly has a historical and thus a chronological series of events to relate. Christianity had great success among women, slaves, and in general among those without power because it offered a message of liberation, that the "powerful" would be "brought down . . . from their thrones" and the "lowly" lifted up (Luke 1:52). Women were present in the upper room after the resurrection, at Pentecost, in the early spirit-filled communities of Christians, and in groups that responded to the missionary work of Peter, Paul, and the others. At Philippi, Thessalonica, Beroea, Athens, Corinth, and Ephesus women responded to the Christian message and became well known, even leaders, in their churches. Not only Luke but his Christian audience knew of these competent women.

But if part of Luke's purpose was apologetic, presenting Christianity to Roman audiences, these noteworthy women are problematic. Roman laws and the general feeling in society in the late first century were disposed toward limiting the influence of women outside the domestic sphere. Luke must tell the Christian story accurately for Christians and yet not present the Jesus movement in ways that would be threatening to the Roman social order. So he mentions the women in Acts but is careful to silence them and to omit or veil any of the technical language of church leadership when describing Christian women. For example, in the stories of Tabitha and Lydia, Luke focuses on the prominence of the women in their communities and hints at their wealth rather than underscoring their contributions as church leaders. As Gail O'Day notes, Luke must present a picture of Christianity that will win the favor of Rome, and in Acts that leads to diminishing the role of women.

BIBLIOGRAPHY

Jervell, J. "The Daughters of Abraham: Women in Acts." In *The Unknown Paul*, 147–57, 186–90. Minneapolis: Augsburg, 1984.

Martin, C. "The Acts of the Apostles." In *Searching the Scriptures*, Volume 2, edited by E. Schüssler Fiorenza, 763–99. New York: Crossroad, 1994.

O'Day, G. "Acts." In *The Women's Bible Commentary*, edited by C. Newsom and S. Ringe, 305–12. Louisville: Westminster/John Knox, 1992.

Reimer, I. *Women in the Acts of the Apostles.* Minneapolis: Fortress, 1995.

Schüssler Fiorenza, E. *In Memory of Her.* New York: Crossroad, 1983.

Thomas, W. "Lydia: A Truely Liberated Woman." *ExpTms* 95 (1984): 112–13.

CONCLUSIONS

A careful reading of Luke-Acts reveals that Luke the evangelist cannot be seen as an unqualified champion of women in early Christianity. He is caught on the horns of a dilemma. He knows that women were indeed prominent in the ministry of Jesus and the spread of Christianity. His community is also aware of these facts and knows the stories of many of the women. On the other hand, he is presenting the Christian gospel to an increasingly conservative Roman Empire, one that has a growing number of women converts who must be catechized. Luke does not want Christians to be understood as practicing un-Roman activities such as prophecy or magic or allowing women public leadership roles. He wants to win Roman acceptance of Christianity, so he must observe the propriety and decorum Rome dictates.

Thus, while Luke multiplies the number of women he mentions, he simultaneously places limits on their function in the community of

Jesus and in the early church. The reforms of Augustus meant that legal marriage had, in Rome, public, communal significance. Public order was maintained by legally ensuring that the household, the sphere to which women belonged, was controlled by men. Luke wants to depict Christian women as respectable within this framework. So the women who most fully receive Jesus' approval are silent (Luke 7:36–50; 10:38–42); virginity is stressed (Luke 2:36–38; Acts 21:9); and Christian women are distanced from prophecy, which the Romans saw as a dangerous manifestation of non-Roman, oriental cults. (Although interestingly in Lukan writings the charism of prophecy is primarily associated with ascetic life-styles, with virgins and widows.)

On several levels, Luke presents a mixed message with regard to women. His writings were intended both to serve for the edification of women converts and to ensure their control. Not unlike what was the case with Paul, while Luke presents a theology of liberation and of equality in Christ, he (who, after all, is traditionally thought to be one of Paul's associates) practically subordinates women to men in the Christian story. As I noted in chapter 3, C. Parvey summarizes the dilemma by saying that Luke has a vision of equality on the theological level but promotes a status quo ethic on the social level ("The Theology and Leadership of Women in the New Testament," in *Religion and Sexism,* edited by R. Radford Ruether [New York: Simon & Schuster, 1974], 146).

But that is not the whole story. In fact there is disparity between what Luke probably intended and how his works have actually been used. As Gail O'Day has pointed out, "glimpses of women's lives and experience slip into the story and work against Luke's aims" ("Acts of the Apostles," in *The Women's Bible Commentary,* 312). The honesty of Luke's presentation has won out over the temporal concerns of his time and community, and we in fact can discern in Luke-Acts the prominence and importance of women in early Christianity. Careful examination of his texts recovers what Luke attempted to exclude. In the final analysis, the Gospel story is not bound by first-century social strictures, even when those who first related it were. "Nothing is covered up that will not be uncovered, and nothing secret that will not become known" (Luke 12:2). What Luke has said in darkness is being exposed to new light, and what he may have wished to whisper behind closed doors is being proclaimed from the housetops of women who have inherited the faith from their foremothers in first-century house-churches.

BIBLIOGRAPHY

D'Angelo, M. "Women in Luke-Acts: A Redactional View." *JBL* 109 (1990): 441–61.

Flanagan, N. "The Position of Women in the Writings of St. Luke." *Marianum* 40 (1978): 288–304.

Parvey, C. "The Theology and Leadership of Women in the New Testament." In *Religion and Sexism,* edited by R. Radford Ruether, 139–46. New York: Simon & Schuster, 1974.

Seim, T. K. *The Double Message: Patterns of Gender in Luke-Acts.* Nashville: Abingdon, 1994.

6

The Deutero-Pauline Texts

METHODOLOGICAL NOTE

A NYONE SETTING OUT TO WRITE on "the New Testament view" of any subject is faced with at least two dilemmas, one chronological and one canonical. The chronological dilemma can be framed by a question. Should the chronology followed be that of the development of early Christianity or of the writings themselves? That is, should one's subject be traced through the history of early Christianity beginning with the life of Jesus and following the spread of the church, in which case one begins with the Gospels, or should the issue be examined in the first books of the New Testament in which it appears, in which case one begins with the Pauline writings, with 1 Thessalonians, and then moves through the subsequent texts.

I have chosen the second approach in this study. After developing a historical and cultural context, we began by looking first at the authentic letters of Paul, the earliest writings in the New Testament, and what they say about women. Then we looked at the Gospels' views, beginning with Mark, the first Gospel to be written, and continuing with John, the last to be composed. Luke and Acts were discussed together because they share a common author. To complete the picture in terms of literary chronology, we are left with the Deutero-Pauline writings. And this leads to the second dilemma.

Toward the end of the first century, disciples of Paul began to adapt his thinking to the changing circumstances of their churches. In a sense, they did what Gospel writers did in adapting the various tradi-

129

tions about Jesus to the communities for which they were writing. These followers of Paul began to produce pseudonymous works, writings under Paul's name but not written by the apostle. This they considered neither dishonest nor plagiarism. Pseudonymity was practiced in the Jewish community in the second and first centuries B.C. (see, e.g., the books of Daniel, Baruch, or Enoch), and was well known in the Greek world as well. (Plato, for example, used Socrates' name.) For a disciple of a great teacher to write a work under the teacher's name was considered a way to honor him, and, conveniently, it gave authority to the work produced. Such writers were not "making things up," but were preserving the thought of their teachers as it applied to new circumstances.

Paul's followers seemed to have employed this common precedent in producing letters in his name. New Testament scholarship agrees that the practice occurred, but evinces little consensus about which New Testament epistles are Deutero-Pauline. Arguing on the basis of differences in literary style, vocabulary, and theological orientation from genuinely Pauline letters, scholars opting for the largest possible Deutero-Pauline canon would include Colossians, Ephesians, 2 Thessalonians, and the Pastoral epistles (1 and 2 Timothy, and Titus). At the very least, most academics now conclude that the Pastoral epistles are pseudonymous. Herein is the second dilemma, a canonical problem. How do we deal with the Deutero-Pauline material? Do we place more emphasis on the authentic writings of Paul and treat the pseudonymous works as genuinely "secondary"? If so, we are creating a "canon within the canon," a list of *more highly* authentic works within the authentic tradition and literary collection of the church. For Christians this presents a real difficulty, since, classically, the *entire* New Testament is considered authoritative. No matter who wrote the Deutero-Pauline works, they are included in the canon of the New Testament and are thus "binding" on Christians.

This fact presents us with a particularly interesting issue in our study of women in the New Testament. As I hope chapter 3 made reasonably clear, Paul does not specifically limit the activity or ministry of women as women in the church. In fact, he knows and approves of the work of women and commends individual women's ministries. The Deutero-Pauline works, on the other hand, seem to recoil from the principle Paul set forth in Gal. 3:28 and exhibit material that is very harsh on and limiting to women. Of the seven strongly "anti-women" passages in the New Testament, only one may be from the hand of

Paul, 1 Cor. 11:3–16 (but see the discussion on this text in chapter 3). One is probably an interpolation into a Pauline letter (1 Cor. 14:34–35); one is found in 1 Pet. 3:1–7, and four occur in the Deutero-Pauline writings (Col. 3:18–19; Eph. 5:22–23; 1 Tim. 2:8–15; and Titus 2:4–5). Some feminist Christian interpreters of scripture have conveniently said something like, "Oh well, these works weren't written by Paul and, therefore, they aren't as binding as Paul's letters." But this creates a "canon within the canon" and ignores the fact that the whole New Testament is considered authoritative by most Christians (and certainly by those who would limit women's roles in the church!).

In the material that follows, I have decided to cast the "pseudonymity net" as widely as possible and include Colossians, Ephesians, 2 Thessalonians, and the Pastoral epistles as Deutero-Pauline. (I realize that many scholars would contest this view, and in fact it represents a departure in my own thinking.) Because of their close literary connection and because they use a number of traditional materials in common, I shall discuss Colossians and Ephesians together, and, as is frequently done in New Testament introductions, treat the Pastorals as a unit. (Because it says nothing specific about women, I omit discussion of 2 Thessalonians.) After having looked at what these letters say to and about women, I explore some reasons why the views set forth in them might be so different from those of the apostle Paul.

INTRODUCTION

All of the authentic letters of the Apostle Paul were probably written before 65 A.D. The Deutero-Pauline texts were written in the last quarter of the first century and the first quarter of the second, roughly from 75 to 125 A.D. By this time a number of significant events had occurred and the situation of the early Christian communities had changed drastically. Paul's authentic epistles had been written and circulated, and Paul and the original Twelve apostles were probably all dead. The disastrous Jewish War of 66–70 had occurred with the results that Jerusalem had been destroyed by the Romans, the Christian and Jewish communities in Judea had been scattered, and the rift between synagogue and church had widened. The Gentile missions of the church were growing and becoming increasingly influential. As a result, the ethnic composition of the church was changing. Second- and third-generation Christians were more likely to be of "pagan," or Greco-

Roman, heritage than of Semitic or Jewish, and thus were unacquainted with the literary and legal traditions of Israel. Traditional Jesus material had been collected, and Mark was written by 70, and Matthew and Luke probably by 85 or 90. The imminently expected parousia, or second coming, of Jesus had not occurred.

As a result of these events, the church's self understanding was changing. Instead of rapturously awaiting the end, the church began to understand that it must survive in history and in the Empire if it was to thrive. At the same time, the church began to face challenges to the teaching of the apostles from within, apparently from those who claimed to follow the Christ, but had not known the historical Jesus, as well as challenges from without, for example, the persecutions of the emperor Domitian (81–96 A.D.), which led to the writing of the book of Revelation. At the same time, Christian theology was increasingly influenced by Hellenism, and in the second century, Gnosticism. To face these challenges, authority and church order became crucially important, and these are the issues that are frequently at the forefront in the Deutero-Pauline texts that address the place of women in the churches.

COLOSSIANS AND EPHESIANS

For a variety of reasons, it is appropriate to discuss Colossians and Ephesians together, not the least of which is that both are addressed to cities in Asia Minor and both seem to come from the same time period and geographical provenance. Whereas Colossians is in form more like a genuinely Pauline epistle and Ephesians is more like a treatise, there is lively debate about the authorship of both, some scholars arguing for Pauline authorship and some disputing it. Both letters exhibit vocabulary, stylistic features, and theological viewpoints that do not occur in the genuinely Pauline epistles. In these and other ways they are more like each other than like other works in the Pauline corpus. Each, for example, is likely to rely more heavily on traditional materials (liturgical fragments, vice and virtue lists, household codes, etc.) than do earlier letters of Paul.

Most tellingly, there is remarkable similarity in the content of the two letters. About a third of the words in Colossians are found in Ephesians, and 73 of the 155 verses in Ephesians have close parallels in Colossians. Many theories exist to explain the similarities. Some scholars have argued that Colossians is Pauline and that a disciple of Paul extensively mined it in the composition of Ephesians. It has been speculated that Ephesians is the letter to the Laodiceans mentioned in Col. 4:16 or is, in fact, a summary of Paul's thought written to conclude an early collection of his letters. While the relationship between the two may never be completely explained, a close reading of Colossians and Ephesians almost certainly confirms some form of literary dependence. [For more complete discussions of the issue see M. Barth, *Ephesians* [Garden City, N.Y.: Doubleday, 1974], 1:36–41; and J. Coutts, "The Relationship of Ephesians and Colossians," *NTS* 4 [1957–58]: 201–7.]

Whoever the author of Colossians was, he had not visited the church (2:1), which seems to have been the result of missionary work in the Lycus valley in the early 50s A.D. The church in Colossae was founded by Epaphras (1:7–8; 4:12–13) and included Onesimus (4:9) and thus Philemon, providing close links with that epistle. References to the past of the Colossian Christians indicates that they were predominantly Gentiles (1:21–22; 2:13). According to the text of the letter, Epaphras brought its author news of threats to the church's faith (1:7–8; 4:12–13) in the form of false teaching called "philosophy" in the letter (2:8). The exact content of the false teaching has engendered lively debate. Whatever it was, the letter's author takes strong exception to it, and the letter itself is primarily written to refute it and those who propound it.

In her essay on Colossians in *Searching the Scriptures*, Volume 2 (New York: Crossroad, 1994), Mary Rose D'Angelo correctly notes that the epistle offers little information on the lives of women in Christian antiquity. It mentions only one woman, Nympha, and, in being the earliest canonical work to employ the *Haustafel*, or household code, it exhibits the first glimpse of an emerging pattern of domination of women, children, and slaves by husbands/fathers/owners in the early Christian communities. It may well be the first step in the creation of a Pauline "school," which appropriated the thought of the surrounding culture in regulating the inner life of the Christian community. But that is to get ahead of ourselves.

Nympha of Colossae appears in 4:15–16, the first of two verses of the letter that give significant information about life in the early Pauline churches. The verses provide a tantalizing but incomplete suggestion of how Paul's letters were collected. At an early stage they were apparently exchanged among the churches and later collated.

Second, it is apparent from 1:24–2:5 that the author intended that the letter be read aloud in the church, and 4:16 makes this explicit. Third, these verses confirm that Christians met together in homes in small groups and that these groups had fellowship with each other.

Nympha herself, like Mary (Acts 12:12) and Lydia (Acts 16:11–15, 40), seems to have been a householder who provided one of the churches in the area with a place to meet. As was the case with Junia in Romans 16 (see chapter 3), there is textual uncertainty about whether "Nympha" is a male or a female name. Some read Nympha as a short form of "Nymphodorus," but note that the contracted form is rare. While it is true that Nympha appears as a woman's name in Latin inscriptions and has been found as a woman's name in Greek literature, textual evidence is divided on whether the pronoun following the phrase containing the name is *autēs* or *autou*. One scholar, remarking on the alternative readings suggests that *autou* is condemned by its simplicity, and *autēs* has arisen because Nympha looks like a woman's name but can hardly be so. But why not? Because the feminine form is unusual? Because a woman could not be the leader of a house-church? This was how Eduard Schweizer read the issue in his *Letter to the Colossians* (Minneapolis: Augsburg, 1976), 241. There he suggests that an original "her" was subsequently changed to "his" because at a later stage in the church's history it could not be conceived that a woman might have been responsible for an entire house-church.

This would not be the first time that a change to a masculine pronoun or name happened in the course of transmission of the New Testament texts (see the discussion of Junia in Romans 16 in chapter 3). Although the textual problem has not been definitively resolved, in my opinion Nympha is another example of a prominent woman in the early church generally, and in the Pauline churches in particular. She was so well known that the author of Colossians could not omit mention of her, even though mentioning her presented certain difficulties for him. Like Lydia, Nympha was head of her own household, which might have included children, relatives, and slaves (see 3:18–4:1). As such, Nympha was a businesswoman of sorts, since she would have been responsible for managing the economic affairs of this household in a building or compound that was large enough to accommodate the meeting of a Christian community.

A female leader of a Christian household presents particular problems for the author of this letter, since in 3:18–4:1 he has previously enjoined the Christians in the area to follow a household code, a particular form of social organization that was rooted in the philosophical politics of Aristotle, which had become the basis of the imperial social policies in the Augustan marital legislation to which we referred previously. Some attention to the form is clearly in order.

The household code is but one example of the practice of the Colossian author of using traditional materials in his epistle. Like vice and virtue lists, the household code is a borrowed literary form that is found extensively in Stoic, Hellenistic Jewish, and early Christian sources. (For an outline of these sources, see chapter 7 of E. Schüssler Fiorenza's *In Memory of Her.*) Its basic ideas can be traced to Aristotle's *Politics* (1.1254b), which argues that the authority of males over females ensures the proper functioning of the household and, by extension, the state. In short, a well-run household is the basis of a well-run state. As is usual in such codes, the first party addressed is subservient to the second, and special attention is given to wives and slaves. Such exhortations generally follow a pattern. The subservient party is addressed, usually in a single word; the command is given, and finally the motivation for obedience is revealed. The number of *hapax legomena* (words that occur only here in the New Testament) in Col. 3:18–24 suggests that the basis of the code existed before it took its present form in the letter. Comparable material in Ephesians 5 and 1 Peter 3 (and in *Didache* 4:9–11; *Barnabas* 19:5–7 and *1 Clement* 21:6–9), passages that are similar in content, vocabulary, and form, have led some scholars to conclude that they come from a common source, probably an early Christian catechetical code of some sort.

As Sarah Tanzer has noted in her article on Ephesians in *Searching the Scriptures*, Volume 2, the codes are important because of the central role of the household in Roman society and the house-church in early Christianity. As we noted in chapter 2, the Roman household included persons who were economically dependent on the master and the spouses and children of that person. The term *paterfamilias* itself suggests that the head of the household was likely to be a male (although we have seen exceptions in female heads of Christian households). All the tasks carried out by the household—work and economic production, education of children, "social security"—were under his control. The household code organized the household in a hierarchical structure of economic dependence. Because early Christianity began in the Greco-Roman world as a household movement, codes organizing households were formative in organizing the church. Whatever their original intention, household codes have played a major part in the later marginalization of women in the church.

Turning, then, to the code in Col. 3:18–4:1, we find that it occurs in the parenetic section of the letter (3:1–4:6) and is framed by material on worship (3:16–17; 4:2–4) just as the limitations placed on women in 1 Corinthians 11 were. In the Colossian church (and in Corinth as well?), where spirit-filled worship occurred (2:18–19) and Christians were under scrutiny from those outside the church, Christians are encouraged to conduct their relationships with appropriate decorum. Since women and slaves apparently present a particular threat of disorder, they are especially addressed by the code and are given theological motivation for their subservience. The code's general purpose is the same as the vice and virtue lists that precede it in 3:1–17—to encourage a certain kind of "Christian" behavior. Whatever Christians do must be done "in the name of the Lord Jesus" (3:17), the injunction that immediately precedes the household code and casts a theological shadow over it. But the weight of the code's injunctions falls on women and slaves.

The household code begins by addressing wives and husbands as the basic unit of the household (3:18–19). As the subordinate party, wives are addressed first and told to "be subject" to their husbands "as is fitting in the Lord." Submission (*hypotassesthe*) is argued on the basis of Christian order as "in the Lord." Whereas in 1 Cor. 7:3–6 Paul thought of marital submission as mutual; here the wife is to be subject to the husband. "As is fitting" suggests that the author accepts the subordination of wives to husband as the appropriate norm. Husbands are to love their wives and are to avoid harshness, *pikrainesthe*, a term implying authoritarian rule. Verses 20 and 21 address children and fathers (note, not mothers or "parents"). Children are to obey their fathers as their "acceptable duty in the Lord" (v. 20). And fathers are to avoid provoking children, a consideration that was perhaps novel in a period in which children were not much esteemed.

Finally, the code addresses the relationship between slaves and masters in 3:22–4:1, the longest section of the code. This is not surprising, since, potentially, Christianity could upset the social balance most dramatically and dangerously with regard to slaves and masters (see Gal. 3:28). Furthermore, the slave Philemon and his master, Onesimus, were from Colossae, so that church had already faced the changes Christianity brought to the slave–master relationship. The writer accepts slavery as a normal part of the social order with no sense that it is morally wrong, and devotes the bulk of his instructions to slaves (vv. 22–25). Like children, slaves are to obey their masters "in everything" and from their inner conviction as Christians rather than from fear of reward or punishment. Christian slaves, the writer implies, work for Christ, not earthly masters, and their reward will come "from the Lord."

Note that the subordinate members of the household—wives, children, and slaves—are given theological motivations for their behavior. Improper behavior on their part (lack of submission, disobedience, sluggardness) will displease not only their husbands/fathers/masters, but the Lord. In contrast, the husbands/fathers/masters are given practical, human motivation for their behavior. The real concern of the Colossian household code is the relationship of subordinate to dominant members of the household. Perhaps this was because women, children, and slaves in the Christian community had more "status" in their households than in the larger society, and they were thus a potential source of criticism of Christianity by that society. The code instructs them to behave in ways that society would find inoffensive and thus not bring attention and censure to Christianity. The author seems to want to ensure that the "otherness" of relationships among Christians is not an affront to the larger society and, as a result, a threat to the Christian community itself.

I think the motivation for the household code in Ephesians is similar. The Ephesian letter presents the interpreter with a number of interesting challenges. Like Corinth, Ephesus was a major city of antiquity, the capital of a Roman province, a major trade center, a religious center, and a crossroads. Ephesus is mentioned at least twenty times in the New Testament. Although Paul did not found the church there, he spent about three years in Ephesus and wrote the majority of his extant letters from that city. But it is unclear whether or not Paul wrote the Ephesian letter. According to the letter, the writer, who is under arrest, does not know those he addresses (1:15; 3:3) and sends one Tychicus to supplement the letter with oral information (3:1–2; 6:20–22). That lack of knowledge seems unlikely if Paul had spent three years in Ephesus.

Textual, literary, linguistic, and stylistic arguments also suggest that Paul did not write Ephesians. The best manuscripts of the epistle do not contain "in Ephesus" in 1:1, and Marcion about 140 A.D. indicated that the letter was the one to the Laodiceans. Many words in the

letter do not appear elsewhere in Paul's writings and words Paul uses
are not used in Pauline ways in Ephesians. The letter contains sentences that are longer and more ponderous than Paul's usually crisp
style. Ephesians exhibits not only dependence on Colossians but on
the earlier, uncontested Pauline letters. Perhaps most telling, the circumstances of the church reflected in Ephesians are not those of Paul's
time. In Ephesians the Jew/Gentile tension so evident in Galatians and
Romans is absent, and the word "church" refers not to believers in a
particular geographical location, but to all believers everywhere.

There are strong counterarguments in favor of the Pauline authorship of Ephesians, and as was the case with Colossians, it may be
impossible ever to establish authorship with certainty. More problematic for interpreters of the letter is that we know almost nothing about
the circumstances of its writing. Some scholars have argued that it is
a letter written to address specific problems in Asia Minor. Others
think it is a summary of Paul's thought written as a "circular letter."
And it has been suggested that Ephesians is not a letter at all, but a
homily or liturgical document. Perhaps little more can be said with
certainty than that Ephesians was written before 95 A.D. (Ephesians
was known to the author of *1 Clement*) in or for a church in Asia Minor
that was primarily Gentile. If it is not written by Paul, it is Pauline in
manner and thought.

Ephesians does not mention any women or address women except
in the context of its expanded household code (5:21–6:9). As in
1 Corinthians 11, Romans 13, Colossians 3, Hebrews 13, James 1, and
1 Peter 2, the themes of subordination and obedience are introduced
after a discussion of worship. In general, this casts a heavy theological
authority over the command to submission, and in the particular case
of Eph. 5:21–6:9 undercuts arguments that the passage is an interpolation. Here 5:21, "Be subject to one another out of reverence of Christ,"
states the principle that governs the whole code. The text falls into
three units: 5:22–33 on wives and husbands; 6:1–4 on children and
fathers; and 6:5–9 on slaves and masters. While all household codes in
the New Testament begin with wives/husbands, marriage is related
here to one of the great themes of the letter, namely, the lordship of
Christ and those who live in union with him, and it is the most
expanded unit of the code.

As in Col. 3:18–4:1, wives are addressed first as the subordinate
party. The words translated "be subject" in English are literally *tois
idiois,* "one's own." The verb for "be subject," *hypotassomai,* does not

appear in Eph. 5:22 but has been carried over from v. 21. Marcus Barth translates v. 22, "wives to your husbands—as to the Lord" (*Ephesians*, vol. 2). Since it is commonly assumed that the writer of Ephesians modeled his work on Colossians, translators seem to have inserted "be subject" in 5:22 to bring it into conformity with Col. 3:18. But it is not in the Greek text. I think that the idea expressed in Eph. 5:22 is closer to that of 1 Cor. 7:2, "each man should have his own wife and each woman her own husband," which encourages mutuality within monogamy, than to Col. 3:18, which enjoins subjection.

While this translation and interpretation soften somewhat the injunction to wives, in 5:22–24 the writer assumes that the household and marital hierarchy of his time parallels an eternal hierarchy. As we noted earlier in this study "head" (*kephalē*) in Hellenistic Greek connotes "source" or "origin" more nearly than "authority" or "ruler." The imagery of Christ as head of the body from 1:22–23 reappears here, so that the husband's headship finds its origin in the lordship of Christ. This means that the husband's authority is analogous to that of Christ, but also that any demand of the husband that is inconsistent with Christ's lordship would be inadmissible.

In fact, the bulk of the instruction in the passage, nine of the twenty-two verses, is directed to the husband, the more powerful of the two parties. His duty is stated in v. 25: he is to love his wife as Christ loved the church and gave himself for her. As a result of the introduction of this comparison, it is unclear in the verses that follow whether what is being discussed is the relationship between the husband and the wife, that between Christ and the church, or both. Verse 32 also makes the reading of vv. 25–33 ambiguous because it leaves us uncertain whether the writer had human marriage or Christ and the church uppermost in mind. In any case, as Sarah Tanzer has pointed out, the Christ–church analogy gives theological justification for the exhortation to wives that is, as she puts it, "more lopsided than mutual."

While husbands are to love their wives as themselves (under the circumstances this can be seen as an alarmingly self-serving motivation, and it certainly contradicts the analogy of Christ and the church), there is no verb applied to husbands that parallels *hypotassō*, "be subject" (or in similar passages in Col. 3:18; 1 Pet. 3:1; 1 Tim. 2:11; or Titus 2:4ff.). Many feminist scholars note that the writer of Ephesians has used Christ to ensure the inferior position of the wife.

The injunctions to children/fathers in 6:1–4 have been expanded from Colossians, but not so extensively as the wives/husbands sec-

tion, and children, along with slaves in 6:5–9, are again given theological motivations for their obedience to their fathers/masters. As was
the case with his view of wives, the author of Ephesians understands
subordination and authority as part of the divine order of the world. A
principle of reciprocity can be seen both here and in the Colossians
household code, although the writer of Ephesians is more explicit in
pointing out that everyone is obedient to someone. The word in 5:21
that introduces the whole section, "submission" (*hypotassamenoi*),
literally means to line up in order, as in the army soldiers lined up and
submitted themselves to the authority of their officers. As soldiers
give up their wills in obedience to their officers, Christians—
wives/husbands, children/fathers, slaves/masters—are to give up their
rights and wills to Christ. Unfortunately, this call for universal submission to Christ has not been heard as clearly as the injunction that
wives submit to husbands, and so the texts have been used to justify
the subjugation of women, slaves, and those with similar social roles
or identities.

Tanzer has pointed out that the household codes in the New Testament may not reflect the actual practice in Roman households so
much as an idealized view of how they *should* function. Certainly they
depict the Christian household as one that *should* be an ordered social
unit under the authority of the ruler of the household. What was at
issue here? Why the move to place women, children, and slaves under
authority? Probably so that Christianity would not be unduly criticized by the larger society.

To limit our discussion to wives, women who did not follow the
social conventions of the day bore the brunt of criticism. Indeed, it was
a standard feature of Hellenistic polemical rhetoric to criticize the
character and/or behavior of a group or movement by criticizing the
behavior of its women. The larger issue was that if Christian women
moved too far beyond the limits of the social conventions of their day,
negative attention would be drawn to the Christian community, and,
ultimately, the gospel would not be heard. Too much freedom for
women (or children and certainly slaves) would create destructive mis-
understanding of the Christians by their Roman neighbors, for whom
well-run households meant a well-run state.

As the enthusiastic expectation of the imminent return of Christ
receded in consciousness, Christians of the late first century were
faced with the challenge of living in Roman society for an extended
period. The greater freedom that in principle was granted to their

women (and the unusual pattern of relationship suggested between Christian masters and slaves) represented a threat to Roman society. The household codes of the New Testament, with their injunction that women be subject, were, at least in part, to see that Christian women were exempt from criticism in the wider society. In fact, the codes encouraged women to conform to the expectations of that society. Thus, the codes represented a retreat from the more emancipated theoretical theological views of Paul and from the practice of Jesus (insofar as we know it from the Gospels).

BIBLIOGRAPHY

Crouch, J. *The Origin and Intention of the Colossian Haustafel.* Göttingen: Vandenhoeck & Ruprecht, 1972.

D'Angelo, M. R. "Colossians." In *Searching the Scriptures,* Volume 2, edited by E. Schüssler Fiorenza, 313–24. New York: Crossroad, 1994.

Johnson, E. "Colossians." In *The Women's Bible Commentary,* edited by C. Newsom and S. Ringe, 346–48. Louisville: Westminster/ John Knox, 1992.

_____. "Ephesians." In *The Women's Bible Commentary,* edited by C. Newsom and S. Ringe, 338–42. Louisville: Westminster/John Knox, 1992.

Lillie, W. "The Pauline Housetables." *ExpTms* 86 [1975]: 179–83.

Moulton, J. H. "Nympha." *ExpTms* 5 (1893–94): 66–67.

Tanzer, S. "Ephesians." In *Searching the Scriptures,* Volume 2, edited by E. Schüssler Fiorenza, 325–48. New York: Crossroad, 1994.

Thurston, B. *Reading Colossians, Ephesians, and II Thessalonians.* New York: Crossroad, 1995.

THE PASTORAL EPISTLES

More attention is devoted to women and their roles in the early church in the Pastoral epistles than in any other section of the New Testament, and a great deal of what is said is either negative or an attempt to limit women's activity. It is this material that has often dominated church teaching with regard to women in subsequent centuries, in part because of the narrative "frame" that has been construed for the

Pastorals. An eighteenth-century German student of the Bible, Paul Anton, called 1 and 2 Timothy and Titus the "Pastoral Epistles," because they appear to be the work of an older pastor giving advice to a younger. For centuries that "advice" has set the normative pattern for church practice.

The primary scholarly question with regard to the Pastorals is authorship. While they contain a great deal of what seems to be autobiographical material about the apostle Paul, the situation of the church that is reflected is much later than what we know of the Pauline churches. Like Colossians, and especially Ephesians, the vocabulary, style, and theology of the Pastoral epistles seem to represent a stage of development beyond Paul, and like those letters they may well belong to Asia Minor. Many scholars now assume that they are pseudonymous epistles (written by someone else and attributed to Paul) written no earlier than the last decade of the first century and perhaps as late as 135 to 150 A.D. The Pastorals contain three kinds of material: apparently biographical information about Paul and Timothy (which is included to establish the authority for the exhortations); polemic against opponents of the writer's positions; and regulations for community life and personal behavior. As we shall see, material dealing with women occurs in each type, although the largest block of material on women is of the last category. If I am correct in my assumption that the Pastorals date from the beginning of the second century and thus depict the church as it moves toward becoming an "institution," then what we see in these epistles are struggles with the chief problems faced by the church in this transitional period: church order, false teaching, and "social acceptability," that is, the church's position in Roman society.

Concern for church order is reflected in the writer's discussion of the offices of ministry. In the Pauline correspondence, ministry is "charismatic," a matter of gifts for service (see 1 Corinthians 11–14). The author of the Pastorals lists qualifications for the offices of bishop, deacon/deaconess, widow, and elder, and presents these ministries from a disciplinary angle. The church had reached a turning point in her understanding of ministry. The reasons for centralizing authority in "offices" included strengthening the unity of congregations and rooting out heresy. Leaders of the church of the second century were aware of threats to the church from within. They apparently thought that the freedom Paul had allowed in ministry needed to be organized and funneled into recognized channels to prevent disunity and heresy.

A second problem, then, was false teaching. Its precise nature has given rise to a great deal of speculative scholarship. The current consensus seems to be that it was some form of Gnosticism to which women were especially attracted. Because they experienced their traditional roles as inadequate or socially marginal, the argument goes, women looked to Gnostic and/or ascetic forms of Christianity for standards of worth more consonant with what they felt were their circumstances. In a very illuminating article, Robert J. Karris has pointed out that in an attempt to inculcate aversion to false teachers, the Pastoral writer borrowed the conventional rhetorical criticism found in popular philosophy (see "The Background and Significance of the Polemic of the Pastoral Epistles," *JBL* 92 [1973]: 549–64). False teachers are called deceivers, quibblers, full of vice, unable to practice what they preach, and quick to prey on women. This is how the false teachers are attacked, but little is said of what they actually taught.

A third problem was the reputation of the church in the larger community, how the church appeared to "outsiders" (see 1 Tim. 2:1–2; 5:14; 6:1–2; Titus 2:1–10). As I have suggested, Christianity's deviations from contemporary social norms threatened *patria*, and thus the whole social fabric. In *The Household of God* (Chico, Calif.: Scholar's Press, 1983), David C. Verner argues that just as the household was the basic unit of society, the church was a social structure modeled on the household. He concludes that social tension related to the household appeared to have centered on the changing roles of women in society. Traditional domestic roles for women were associated on a symbolic level with the preservation of an orderly society. Groups whose behavior defied tradition risked the charge of political subversion. Enter Christianity, with its message of equality and freedom! In order to avoid conflict with the Empire, the church at the end of the first century began to conform to Roman social norms. This is particularly evident in the admonitions to women in the Pastorals. As the church clamped down on their "freedom in Christ," women attracted by that freedom moved into communities which they believed preserved the original spirit of Christianity.

Church order, false teaching, and the tenuous position of the church in society after the severity of Domitian form the backdrop for the material on women in the Pastoral epistles. In what follows, we shall examine that material under three headings: women mentioned by name, directives given to women, and women in the "offices" of the early church.

Women are mentioned by name in the Pastoral epistles only in 2 Timothy. Like the apparently biographical material on Paul and Timothy, the named women present an interesting problem in connection with the question of authorship. If the Pastorals were written as much as forty or fifty years after the genuine Pauline epistles, why do they contain "characters" who also appear in the earlier works? The simplest answer is that they function as part of the "framing" of the Pastorals, whose writer mentions them, as he does Paul and Timothy, to provide a traditional and authoritative context for his polemic and injunctions. But this causes an interesting dilemma.

2 Timothy mentions Prisca (Priscilla) and Aquila (4:19), Lois and Eunice (1:5), and Claudia (4:21). Prisca and Aquila are greeted by the Pastoral writer and can hardly be a couple other than the one mentioned in the Corinthian correspondence (1 Cor. 16:29) and Romans (16:3–5; see also Acts 18:2–3, 18, 26). They apparently were Christians in Rome who were expelled by Claudius's decree in 48/49 A.D., who migrated to Corinth, where they joined Paul's mission, and subsequently moved with him to Ephesus. Prisca's name is usually presented before her husband's, indicating that she was of higher social status than he or was more prominent in the early church (some writers have suggested that it was she who corrected and instructed Apollos) or both. We noted earlier in this work that Prisca and Aquila were but one of a number of missionary couples in the early church, and that Prisca was the more prominent Christian teacher. As such she is a difficulty for the Pastoral writer; he wants to establish authenticity and credibility for his work by mentioning the couple, but by doing so he reminds his readers of a woman who does not really follow the injunctions given to women in, for example, 1 Tim. 2:11–15, a text in which women are forbidden to teach. Apparently his desire for establishing historical credibility outweighed his need for strict consistency.

Lois and Eunice (2 Tim. 1:5) are apparently more "useful" examples of Christian womanhood for the Pastoral writer, since as mothers they exemplify his teaching that women "will be saved through childbearing, provided they continue in faith and love and holiness, with modesty" (1 Tim. 2:15). Lois is the mother of Eunice and the grandmother of Timothy. Both women are commended for their Christian faith, a faith Timothy is encouraged to keep. The Pastoral writer seems to imply that Timothy received his faith from his foremothers. Apparently they taught the faith to their male child . . . even though the

Pastoral writer says, "I permit no woman to teach or to have authority over a man" (1 Tim. 2:12).

Little can be known about Claudia (2 Tim. 4:21), who is one of four Christians who apparently sent greetings to the recipients of 2 Timothy. Her name suggests that she was a member of the imperial household, perhaps a slave, or a member of the *gens Claudia*. A Claudia is mentioned in the Apostolic Constitutions (7.46); there she was the mother, or possibly the wife, of Linus, the first bishop of Rome. It has also been argued that Claudia and Pudens were husband and wife and that Linus was their son, but that is problematic since Linus is named between his "parents" in 2 Timothy. Another ancient tradition suggests (perhaps on the basis of a couple by that name in Martial's *Epigrams*, 4:13) that Claudia married Pudens. Both male names preceded hers in 2 Timothy; if she were married to either then we have another of the missionary couples who worked in the Pauline churches.

As was the case in the genuinely Pauline epistles, the Pastoral epistles indicate that women were not only present but prominent in Pauline and post-Pauline churches. The fact that their names survive in the Pastorals indicates their importance, since, in essence, the teaching material in those epistles seeks to limit the participation of women in the community, and since therein women have a tendency to be referred to unflatteringly. Mention is made of "profane myths and old wives tales" (1 Tim. 4:7) and of "silly women, overwhelmed by their sins and swayed by all kinds of desires" (2 Tim. 3:6).

The directives to women in the Pastorals fall into two primary blocks of material, 1 Tim. 2:8–15 and Titus 2:3–5. As were the household codes in Colossians and Ephesians, the injunctions to women in 1 Tim. 2:8–15 occur in the larger context of worship and prayer. (The passage is, not surprisingly, often linked with 1 Cor. 14:34–36.) After instructing all Christians to pray for "kings and all who are in high positions" (2:2), and Christian men to pray "lifting up holy hands without anger or argument" (2:8), the writer launches into injunctions to women that instruct them to dress modestly, to be silent and submissive, and to stop teaching.

The instructions about dress, that women should "dress themselves modestly and decently in suitable clothing, not with their hair braided, or with gold, pearls, or expensive clothes" (2:9), indicates that there were wealthy women in the Pastoral churches, women who had money and leisure for hairdressers and jewelry. At least one interpreter of this passage thinks that the instructions here are directed only to these wealthy women, who are the prime targets of greedy, false teachers (see 1 Tim. 3:1–9). The restrictions thus would be understood to be temporary and binding only on a particular group of women.

But it seems to me that the real focus of the passage is not dress but the women's behavior in general and in the Christian community. Twice they are told to be silent, to "learn in silence" (v. 11) and "to keep silent" (v. 12), and they are not permitted 'to teach or to have authority over a man" (v. 12). The word for "silence" here, *hēsychia*, in Greek means more nearly "in quiet manner" or "with a quiet demeanor," suggesting that the issue was some form of disruptive behavior, perhaps like the anger and argumentativeness of the men alluded to in v. 8, or ecstatic behavior like that associated with pagan religious practice. Commentators, however, have usually read it to mean not that women must learn and participate quietly, but that they must not speak at all.

On the basis of the order of creation, the writer argues that a woman must not teach or have authority over a man (vv. 13–14). This is a *haggada* on Genesis which asserts that women must be submissive because of their role in the fall (see Paul's treatment of the same theme in 2 Cor. 11:2–3, 14). Why an appeal to Hebrew scripture? What was at issue? If recent scholarship is correct, and the theological problem in the churches of the Pastorals was Gnostic influence, the situation becomes clearer. The Gnostics may well have encouraged Christian women to lead in worship and teaching. Their suspicion of the physical would have led them to ignore what the Pastoral writer obviously felt was the importance of physical differences between men and women and perhaps to have been suspicious of marriage itself. The Pastoral writer wants to ensure the traditional hierarchy of the patriarchal household and the traditional maternal role for women.

And herein, as Linda Maloney has pointed out, he makes a serious theological error himself. The Pastoral writer states that a woman "will be saved through childbearing." On the face of it, this suggests that Christ's redemptive and saving work does not extend to women; they must save themselves by a particular form of "work." But certainly this flies in the face of all that Paul has said about the question in Galatians and Romans. In an attempt to speak to what really affronted him, women's leadership as authoritative teachers in the church, the Pastoral writer oversteps himself theologically. But it is injunctions to silence and submission and not his grave theological error that subsequent generations have remembered.

The injunctions to women in Titus 2:3–5 are directed specifically to mature women and occur in a larger context that is reminiscent of a household code, although the "household" here seems to be the church community. The writer speaks to older men (2:2), older women (2:3–5), younger men (2:6–8), and slaves (2:9–10); young women are mentioned only in connection with what the older women will teach them. The writer begins by reminding older women to be reverent, honest, and sober, and to *teach* "what is good" (v. 3). They are to encourage young women to love husbands and children, to be self-controlled and chaste, good household managers, and submissive to their husbands—in short, to be model Roman matrons. Nothing in the list is specifically Christian except the motivation for action, "so that the word of God may not be discredited" (v. 5). The concern seems to be for what those outside the church will think of it.

Interestingly, there is a close correspondence between the qualities required of older women here and those required for deaconesses in 1 Tim. 3:11. It is assumed that young women will be married (a curious assumption in light of Paul's preference for singleness in 1 Corinthians 7), although their behavior here again is remarkably like that laid out for young widows in 1 Tim. 5:14. The older women are to teach the younger women domestic virtues. The assumption that young women are married effectively exempts them from the celibate order of widows and its tasks. This similarity between the behavior expected of older women and deaconesses and younger women and young widows leads directly to the third block of material on women in the Pastorals, that outlining the "orders," or church offices, that women apparently assumed.

Following the instructions on prayer and worship, which contain the restrictions on women (2:1–15), 1 Timothy begins a list of qualifications for specific offices in the church (3:1–7, bishops; 3:8–13 deacons; 5:3–16, widows; 5:17–22, elders) and a discussion of ministry in general (4:6–16). At least one of the offices included women—deacons—and one was specifically for women—widows. The qualifications for deacons are given in 3:8–13. Having listed the fundamental dos and don'ts for deacons in vv. 8–10, the Pastoral writer begins v. 11 "women likewise must be serious, not slanderers, but temperate, faithful in all things." Standard translations of the verse have rendered the first word, *gynaikas,* as "wives," and thus readers have assumed these are instructions to the wives of the male deacons. But the first dictionary definition of *gynē* in Greek is "woman," not "wife." Thus, the *diakonoi* of the passage are both men and women.

This reading is borne out by a parallel reference in the genuine Pauline corpus, Rom. 16:1–2, with its mention of Phoebe the *diakonos* of Cenchreae. (And some scholars have suggested that the women mentioned in Philippians were also deacons, although that term, which first appears in the New Testament in Phil. 1:1, is not used of them in the text of the letter.) Furthermore, if the women in 1 Tim. 3:11 are the wives of the deacons, why are no instructions given to the wives of the bishops? In genuinely Pauline letters deacons seemed to be a special class of Paul's co-workers who were active in preaching and teaching and who were entitled to the esteem and financial support of their congregations. Certainly "deaconesses" are represented in the later church orders like the Apostolic Constitutions, the Didascalia Apostolorum, and the Canons of Hippolytus. What we seem to have in 1 Tim. 3:11 is a listing of injunctions to deaconesses that are roughly parallel to those given to deacons in 3:8–9. I would suggest, then, that the instructions in vv. 12–13 are directed to both the male *and* female deacons—"who serve well as deacons gain a good standing for themselves and great boldness in the faith that is in Christ Jesus" (v. 13). The existence of this order of deaconesses stands in strong contrast to the restrictions placed on women in 1 Tim. 2:9–15 (more on that point presently).

1 Timothy 5:3–16 presents the interpreter with a number of interesting questions. Many of our modern difficulties with this text on widows arise because the author is not instituting new practices but limiting existing ones. There are two general approaches to the text. The first holds that it has three sections: vv. 3–8 on the care of widows; v. 9, which begins a new section on requirements for the office of widow; and v. 16, which stands alone as a distinct injunction. The second interpretation argues that vv. 3–16 are a unified whole defining a "real widow." Both readings imply two groups, widows enrolled in an order and widows ineligible for enrollment because of family connection, age, or wealth. My contention is that the passage discusses three groups: "real widows" in vv. 3, 5–7, 9–10; widows not enrolled in the order because they have some other means of support (vv. 4, 8, 16); and the problematic group of younger widows in vv. 11–15 who might require financial support but could not, because of age, be enrolled.

Questions are sometimes raised about the existence of an order of widows. Key arguments supporting an order include the context in 1 Timothy, the terms *tima* and *katalegestho*, and the suggestion that a vow or pledge was taken upon admittance. The widows do appear in a roster of church offices, which suggests that widows are one of those offices. In v. 3 *tima* in its general meaning is "honor," "respect," or "value," but it also means "pay" or "compensate," and in later church orders the word is used as a technical term for payment. (In the Septuagint Ecclesiasticus uses *tima* in this sense: "Honor the physician with the honor due him" [38:1].)

Katalegestho in v. 9 means "enroll." In parallel literature it is used as a technical term for the registration of levied troops, and it can mean to be adopted into a fellowship by election. Finally, although it occurs in the material on younger widows, "their first pledge" (v. 12), refers to the oath of celibacy taken by widows at their enrollment into the order. The phrase expresses more than resolution; it is used regularly in legislative formulations and official decrees in the period. While none of these elements alone provides conclusive proof of an order, taken together they are a classic case of the whole being more than the sum of the parts. In addition, widows, like deaconesses, are clearly listed among the orders in later church documents. Furthermore, the text lists requirements for enrollment in an order and suggests tasks its members performed.

To be enrolled, a real widow must be alone (dependent on God and not other persons), must be continually faithful, and must be chaste (vv. 5–7). Verse 9 begins "let a widow be put on the list" suggesting that qualifications will follow. And they do: age, marital status, and the general requirement that she has performed good deeds. Each requirement relates to one of the problems we have noted in the church of the Pastorals. The faithfulness and chastity mentioned in vv. 5–6 reflect the preoccupation of the non-Christian world with continence. In Cynic-Stoic diatribes, continence is crucial to the ideal of the detached "wise man." In Neoplatonism, asceticism reached its highest point; the first perfection was to subdue the body. Evidence for the lofty regard for virginity in the early church is clear in the New Testament itself (see, e.g., Matt. 19:29; 1 Cor. 7:7–9, 32–34). The command that widows be chaste is a case in point of the church's concern for society's opinion of her. Verse 6 may well reflect the fear that widowhood might lead to prostitution, as well it might if the widow had no family or means of support. And the command *paraggelle* (v. 7) underlines the fact that the church's conduct must be above reproach. While all Christians should be free of reproach, it is especially important that this be true of those who hold office in the church and of Christian women, who were the special objects of criticism by opponents of Christianity.

Sixty is set as the age of enrollment for widows, probably because it was understood as the age of the "elderly" in ancient literature (see Plato's *Laws* 6.759d). Furthermore, as we have noted, it was the practice for men to marry much younger women, so there were young widows who by Roman law should remarry and by Christian standards would require guidance. A woman of sixty was thought to have ripe experience of life and to be at less sexual peril as she carried out the duties of the order, duties that could be exercised without undue physical exertion. That the widow is to have been the wife of one husband is, again, tied to contemporary norms (compare 1 Tim. 3:2 and 12). A frequent character in ancient literature is the figure of the flighty widow who moves from her dead husband into a series of relationships (see the matron of Ephesus in Petronius's *Satyricon*). Such a woman was an object of scorn. In the Roman world *univira* was an epithet for a good wife and, from a term used to praise a once-married woman, *univira* came to connote chastity for the love of God. In short, once-married persons preserved the church's reputation and moral standing in the wider community.

Continence, age, and marital status as qualifications for "real widows" are followed by evidence of a life of active service. Verse 10 opens and closes with "doing good." The examples given of good works are domestic activities, bringing up children, and showing hospitality, behavior expected of all females (compare Titus 2:3–5). Karen Torjesen has studied extensively the relationship between the Greco-Roman household and the early church and has noted that leadership roles in the church were based on parallel roles in the household. The good deeds of v. 10 can all be seen as those of household management (a requirement for both bishops and deacons; compare 3:4, 12); each qualified a woman for leadership in the church. So long as her office was associated with proper female duties in the *oikos*, the household, the larger society would not be affronted.

Having listed qualifications for the office of widow, the Pastoral writer only suggests its special duties. Interestingly, the widow is to have performed diaconal duties before she is enrolled. Perhaps they are to continue. Several responsibilities are implied. The first is prayer and intercession. Studies of the early church have noted that elderly Christians were encouraged to lead contemplative lives. Physical deterioration precluded more active service; anyone could pray. Since destitution was a primary qualification for the order of widows, they had no material means for benevolence. And freedom from domestic duties gave them more time for devotion. The final reason for their office of prayer was theological. The Jewish tradition taught that God's ears were especially tuned to hear persons totally dependent upon God. God promised to be the special advocate and protector of widows. God's preference was for the poor and destitute (see Sirach 35:14, 17).

While teaching does not appear here as a duty, there is textual evidence in the Pastoral epistles for suggesting that it was one of the widows' tasks. Recall that Titus 2 deals with the promotion of sound doctrine. It addresses older men, older women, young men, and slaves. Older women were to serve the church by teaching the younger women acceptable female behavior: sensibility, chastity, domesticity, kindness, submissiveness to husbands (Titus 2:4–5). These older women (*presbytas*), whom some scholars have associated with the widows, must have lived these lessons in order to be enrolled.

What can we conclude, then, about the order of widows in the Pastoral epistles? The Pastoral writer was apparently limiting an existing order; he gives little information about its duties, assuming that his readers know them. Since we do not, we must speculate. The widows were called to live lives of prayer. They probably taught younger women, and they may have made pastoral house calls. Requirements for the order included that a woman have no other means of support, that she be at least sixty years of age and the wife of one husband, and that she have attested good deeds (of domesticity, hospitality, humility, and compassion). She took a vow of enrollment by which she pledged lifelong fidelity to the order, to Christ, and to the church.

The problem group in the passage is young widows. They bring into focus the attitude of the larger society toward the church ("so as to give the adversary no occasion to revile us" [v. 14]) and the problem with false teaching ("they learn to be idle, gadding about from house to house, and . . . also gossips and busybodies" [v. 13]). No charges against the church were so effective as those brought against the character of its women. By excluding young widows from the order, the writer is, in effect, encouraging them to remarry, to observe Roman law, to follow the societal and legal expectations of women of their age. Thus, the reputation of Christianity would be protected.

The sexuality of young widows was potentially problematic to the church in at least two ways. First, they might not remain celibate or chaste; they might engage in active sexual relationships, thereby shaming the church (compare 1 Corinthians 5). Second, we know from other sources that one of the prominent features of what the Pastoral writer referred to as false teaching was sexual asceticism (see E. A. Clark, "Ascetic Renunciation and Feminine Advancement: A Paradox of Late Ancient Christianity," *Anglican Theological Review* 63 [1981]: 240–57). Some young widows apparently found this asceticism appealing and, furthermore, enrollment in the order would offer them a certain degree of emancipation from domestic responsibility. While celibacy was required by the order, a woman was thereby freed from other restrictions, and she received some form of support from the church community. As the church adapted to society's norms with regard to regulation of its households, applicants for the widow's order increased as women sought a degree of freedom. The growing size of the order was met by the Pastoral writer with injunctions and limitations drawn from societal norms, and criteria for enrollment in the order which affirmed the very behavior from which some widows, by virtue of their enrollment, hoped to be exempt: domesticity, marital fidelity, childbearing, and child-rearing.

In hindsight, we see two paradoxes here. First, when the church followed the household model women had more positions of authority because they had more responsibility *in* the household. But household duties severely limited the sphere of women's activity. So women sought to escape the household by means of the widow's order with the "catch-22" that household management and domestic responsibility were requirements for entrance into the order.

By the time the Pastoral epistles were written, the order of widows had apparently grown large and vigorous. (And, as later church ordinances attest, the order continued in prominence well into the fourth century.) It attracted a variety of women, some of whom apparently abused their position in the church. Therefore the writer of the Pastorals set requirements for enrollment that were strict enough to limit the number of enrolled widows (and thus relieve the financially burdened church? Compare Acts 6:1-6), to prevent the embarrassment caused when the younger widows broke their pledge by remarrying or trespassing society's norms for them, and to limit the number of older women "telling tales." The goal was apparently reduction of the group by selecting those widows most in need of support and those exhibiting the domestic virtues of which Roman society approved.

In conclusion, then, feminist scholarship reminds us that the Pastorals are not primarily descriptive but prescriptive; they are attempting to change existing situations. Rhetorically their polemic reflects the standard modes of attack on opponents, not necessarily the positions held by those opponents. The fact that a relatively large amount of space is devoted to prescribing norms for women's behavior suggests that women were prominent in the Christian community to which the Pastorals are addressed. Women's activity and leadership in the community are what concerned the writer, who sought to place limits on what was an important and influential group in the church.

BIBLIOGRAPHY

Bassler, J. M. "The Widow's Tale: A Fresh Look at I Tim. 5:3–16." *JBL* 103 (1984): 23–40.

Besancon-Spencer, A. D. "Eve at Ephesus." *JETS* 17 (1974): 215–22.

Karris, R. J. "The Background and Significance of the Polemic of the Pastoral Epistles." *JBL* 92 (1973): 549–64.

MacDonald, D. "Virgins, Widows, and Paul in Second Century Asia Minor." In *SBL 1979 Seminar Papers*, Volume 1, edited by P. Achtemeier, 169–84. Missoula, Mont.: Scholars Press, 1979.

Maloney, L. "The Pastoral Epistles." In *Searching the Scriptures*, Volume 2, edited by E. Schüssler Fiorenza, 670–89. New York: Crossroad, 1994.

Padgett, A. "Wealthy Women at Ephesus: I Tim. 2:8-15 in Social Context." *Interpretation* 41 (1987): 19–31.

Thurston, B. "Pastoral Epistles." In *Dictionary of Feminist Theology*, edited by L. Russell and J. Clarkson, 203–4. Louisville: Westminster/John Knox, 1996.

——. *The Widows: A Women's Ministry in the Early Church*. Minneapolis: Fortress, 1989.

Verner, D. *The Household of God*. Chico, Calif.: Scholars Press, 1983.

CONCLUSIONS

We noted in the chapter on Paul's letters that the apostle's own views with regard to women were ambiguous. On the one hand, he set forth a principle of equality in Christ (Gal. 3:28) and commended the work of numerous women he knew in the churches with which he was associated. But, on the other, he never questioned the structures of society that led to the oppression of women; and in practice his tendency was to recommend social roles for women that, in effect, led to their subordination, or at least their second-class status.

The Deutero-Pauline authors attempted to use Paul's letters as a sort of blueprint for the later churches. William O. Walker, Jr. has argued that a postapostolic "Paulinist" wing of the church in fact reacted against Paul's own egalitarianism. We see their thought in passages like 1 Cor. 14:34–35; Col. 3:18–19; Eph. 5:22–23; and the Pastoral epistles. Walker thinks the primary concern of these passages was the domestic status of women and their relationship to their husbands, their religious status and role in the life of the church, and the proper attire and demeanor of women. These Paulinist passages are dominated by patriarchalism, and outside them there is nothing in the New Testament to support male domination and female subordination.

While Walker's position has much to commend it, I think it is a little facile. It seems to me too easy to say, in effect that Paul was pro-woman, but the Deutero-Paulinists were not. The changing circumstances of the church from the mid-first century to the early second need to be taken into account. At the very least, early in his career, Paul and his churches expected the immediate return of the Lord Jesus. They were not concerned with maintaining or changing any social order, or even particularly with their place in the existing one. By the end of the century it began to be apparent that the parousia might not be imminent, in which case the church was in for a "longer haul," and thus needed to face the issue of its position in the Empire. By the beginning of the second century, the Christians in the Empire had faced persecution precisely because they were Christians. Leaders of the church were faced with the possibility of persecutions that could effectively wipe out Christianity. Coarsely put, the choice was between radically living out the implications of Paul's theology and thereby incurring the wrath of an Empire powerful enough to destroy Christianity or quietly trying to find a balance between accepted and acceptable social norms and Christian teaching, thereby preserving the Gospel. Faced with this dilemma, at least some Christian leaders/authors opted to try to form the emerging church according to patterns the Empire found acceptable. Most of the limiting injunctions on women in the Deutero-Pauline texts seem to me to be directed to precisely these circumstances.

Knowing the historical circumstances of their origins, however, does not mitigate the damaging effect these texts have had on women in the church in subsequent centuries. Those whose agenda has been to limit the role of women in home, society, and church have paid little attention to the subtleties of *Sitz im Leben* (setting in life), and passages from the Deutero-Pauline writings have been used prescriptively and with devastating effect. It is at precisely this point that a traditional understanding that the *whole* canon of the New Testament is authoritative for Christians comes into conflict with a position commonly held by feminist interpreters, that no text of scripture that limits or diminishes the personal worth of women as women (or anyone as person-before-God) can be the revealed word of God.

BIBLIOGRAPHY

Pagels, E. "Paul and Women." *JBL* 42 (1974): 538–49.
Walker, W. "The 'Theology of Woman's Place' and the 'Paulinist' Tradition." *Semeia* 28 (1983): 101–12.

7

Perplexities, Trajectories, and Conclusions

A S I INDICATED IN THE INTRODUCTION to this book, its purpose is to give an overview of women as they appear in the text of the New Testament and, in the process, to summarize some of the current scholarly discussion about the texts introduced. I have not aspired to be either comprehensive (I did not, for example, treat Matthew's Gospel, 1 Peter, Hebrews, or the Revelation to John) or inclusive (feminist and other scholarly works that are not included here treat the same texts that we examine). I did strive to present a wide range of materials and opinions. In light of those disclaimers, then, a conclusion would be fatuous. Rather I close this work by sharing some of the perplexities I struggle with in light of the material presented and by suggesting some trajectories, some directions the materials seem to move us in and some directions future scholarship might take.

One of the things I hope my book has made clear is how important it is to read a text in light of its author's presuppositions and goals. Not only biblical narratives but, I would argue, all the texts of the New Testament must be read with attention to the author's purposes. What is the writer trying to accomplish by telling this piece of the Jesus story? What is his or her purpose in writing this letter to this church in this way? Who benefits from the telling of the story or the teaching in the epistle? And who is disadvantaged by it? This asks us not only to assume a "hermeneutics of suspicion," to assume that more may be at work than meets the eye, but a "hermeneutics of context," and context on two levels. First, we must be mindful of the literary context, the location of our text in its surrounding materials and its own genre and the resulting literary issues. Second, we must be mindful of the social, cultural, and theological context, the *Sitz im Leben* (setting in life), of the author. Finally, of course, we must be as honest as we can possibly be about our *own* presuppositions. (I, for example, indicated in the introduction that I am a Christian writing within the church. But that does not make me either blind or uncritical.)

With this in mind, perhaps the primary perplexity this study has left me with is that of the relationship between the Gospels and the Deutero-Pauline canon, and this is a two-sided perplexity. The first side addresses a composition history problem. Recall that most scholars would concur that the Gospels were written between 60 and 110 A.D., with the majority of the material falling between 70 and 90. Matthew, Luke, and John probably were written between 85 and 95, or roughly at the same time that the first contributions to the Deutero-Pauline canon were being introduced to the churches. Matthew, Luke, and John were written at roughly the same time as Colossians and Ephesians, and it may well be that Luke and John share a geographical origin with those epistles. Now think about the view of women, and especially of women and family life, in those works (review chapters 4, 5, and 6 of this book).

In the Gospel of John women are presented as full dialogue partners with Jesus, faithful disciples, and models of Christian behavior. Even with the reservations we introduced in chapter 5, Luke's Gospel and the Acts of the Apostles, which was written at about the same time, introduce a large cast of women characters of whom Jesus approves and whom the early church remembered and honored in its own storytelling. Colossians and Ephesians, on the other hand, employ for the first time the household codes, regulations ordering the Christian household along Greco-Roman lines, which, effectively, limited Christian women. John and the Pastoral epistles may have been written at about the same time, but how differently they present appropriate Christian womanhood.

This fact of composition history makes me wonder how the early Christians who first encountered this body of material reacted. Did they puzzle over the disparity in the views of women that the works presented, or is that a modern concern? Did Christian women at the end of the first century look to their communities' gospels and epistles for guidance and find conflicting information? And this musing led me to the side 2 of this perplexity, the very different views of family life that these particular books of the New Testament present.

The issue was brought into sharp focus for me by Carolyn Osiek's presidential address at the fifty-eighth meeting of the Catholic Biblical Association of America in 1995 (subsequently published as "The Family in Early Christianity: 'Family Values' Revisited," *CBQ* 58 [1996]: 1–24). Osiek pointed out that while Jesus evinces interest in the family life of others, he eschews family life for himself, and, in fact, he initiates a new model of family based on discipleship. He "resets the boundaries of kinship." The things Jesus says and does in relation to what we moderns call the "nuclear family" (a family model unknown in the Greco-Roman world) are disturbing to say the least. As a twelve-year-old, Jesus ignores parental worry to tarry in the Temple. When he is a young man, his family thinks he may be mentally ill (Mark 3:20), and he responds by questioning their ability to discern the Holy Spirit (Mark 3:28–30). At their second attempt to bring him home, Jesus rejects blood kinship ties altogether in favor of the "family" created by his followers (Matt. 13:55–56; Mark 6:3; Luke 4:22; John 6:42). At Cana, Jesus ignores maternal authority (although he later fulfills Mary's request; see John 2). When a woman in a crowd praises Jesus' mother for his birth and nurture, he responds, "Blessed are those who hear the word of God and keep it" (Luke 11:27–28). As troubling as it is to us, Jesus consistently places the demands of the gospel above the duties of the family, and he warns his followers of the disruption that their loyalty to him will cause within their biological families (Matt. 10:21; Mark 13:12). Loyalty to Jesus will pit family members against each other, and those who love family more than they love him and his message are not worthy of the kingdom he proclaims.

Compare this line of teaching with that which we encountered in the Deutero-Pauline writings. Or consider that 1 Pet. 3:1–2 tells a believing wife that her husband may be won to Christianity by her submissive, reverent behavior, while Mark 10:29-30 assumes that the disciples have left the family community altogether. The question that Osiek suggests this raises is whether Christianity promoted harmonious relationships in the recognized social structure of the Greco-Roman family or represented a shocking challenge to that most cherished human relationship. At about the same time, New Testament writers are both advocating family structures that conformed to patriarchal hierarchies and attributing to Jesus the rejection of primary loyalty and allegiance being given to the family. No wonder the writers of the Deutero-Pauline canon felt they needed to allay fears that Christians would subvert the social order! Why did the Deutero-Pauline view triumph? Why, in the words of Luise Schottroff, for centuries has Cicero triumphed over Jesus in the interpretation of the New Testament? (see *Lydia's Impatient Sisters* [Louisville: Westminster/John Knox, 1995], part IV section 2).

For me, at least this makes discussions that are sometimes considered dry or "only scholarly" very pressing indeed. Where *were* Luke and John written, and when? Who *did* write Colossians, Ephesians, and the Pastoral epistles, and when and where were they written? I hope these are questions that feminist scholars will take up in an attempt to speak to the very complex issue of the place of the Christian woman in the family and the larger society.

And this leads to a second perplexity, or perhaps just to a reiteration of what may be the obvious: the picture that the New Testament gives us of women is multicolored, multidimensional, polystylistic—in short, varied. The earliest records we have of women in Christian communities, the authentic letters of Paul, don't even attempt to give objective accounts of the lives of women in Corinth or Philippi or Rome. Information is there, but it is usually cloaked in either a theological discussion or a prescriptive passage—Paul telling women what they *ought* to do—and from that we must struggle to discern what they actually *did* do. Or consider the Gospels. Mark's concern to encourage a Gentile-Christian community enduring persecution is quite different from Luke's apologetic intent to present Christianity favorably to the Romans. John's primary concern seems to be Christology, and that colors his presentation of all the characters in his Gospel. Essentially they are "foils" for Jesus. All of this is to say that the materials from which we construct a picture of women in the New Testament are multifarious. Another trajectory that scholarship on women in the New Testament needs to continue to pursue, then, is that of treating carefully questions related to the composition history, genre, and authorial intent of the source material.

Yet in spite of all the complexity and perplexity encountered, when I sit back and reflect on it, I am struck again by the sheer volume of material on women in the New Testament. In an age and culture that did not take women particularly seriously, for me this in itself is cause for celebration. I can name numbers of women who knew Jesus and who were leaders in the early church. I know for certain that women were strong and outspoken and vigorous enough in some Christian communities, that the male leaders of those communities worried about (and sometimes tried to limit and silence) them. I know that much of the language and terminology used of male leaders in early Christian communities was also used in connection with females. I rejoice that Paul, who is often viewed as opposed to women, knew, greeted, commissioned for service, and approved of women in positions of leadership in churches he founded and/or served. I agree with what seems to me the balanced conclusion of Howard Clark Kee in *Christian Origins in Sociological Perspective* (Philadelphia: Westminster, 1980) that while the New Testament evidence is not sufficient to suggest the full equality of men and women in the church, the prominence given to women is an unusual feature of social movements of the early Empire.

While the New Testament has passages that express disdain for women, on balance there are a striking number of ways in which women are valued. John the Baptist preached to them and baptized them. Jesus not only raised the status of women but put them on equal spiritual footing with men. Acts reports that large numbers of men and women joined the Jesus movement, and both were persecuted and imprisoned for their decision. Paul commends the work of women "fellow workers," and even the Deutero-Paulinists recognized, albeit negatively, their leadership. If all this is so, and I hope this study has demonstrated that it is, what happened?

In writing this book I have come back again and again to Constance Parvey's insight in her 1974 essay "The Theology and Leadership of Women in the New Testament" (in *Religion and Sexism*, edited by R. Radford Ruether [New York: Simon & Schuster, 1974]). She noted that the New Testament gives two messages with regard to women. First, it presents a theology of equality in Christ, a vision of equality on the theological level. But in practical parenesis many New Testament passages support women's subordination; that is, they present a status quo ethic on the social level. I find her analysis fundamentally correct. Part of the power of Jesus' proclamation of the reign of God had to do with the fact that it ushered in an entirely new mode of human existence. The fact that Jesus himself broke boundaries in his dealings with people led his disciples to challenge those same boundaries in their dealings with each other. Why, after all, did they matter? The Lord was soon to return to establish his kingdom. As time passed and the church lost its sense that the kingdom was imminent, it seems to have lost the thinking and will to live as if the kingdom was at hand. And society's boundaries and its shoulds and oughts crept into church teaching and, alas, diminished its gospel proclamation.

I began the introduction of this book with the not very irenic metaphor of land mines. I rather hope a few have been set off in your mind as you read the book and that you thought carefully about why that particular issue was explosive for you. The most explosive issue here, the one underlying them all, it seems to me, is Jesus' proclamation by deed and word of the reign of God. As I read the Gospels, under the reign of God men and women are intended to live and to work together in a discipleship of equals. In the Philippian letter, Paul presented this discipleship of equals in terms of mutual humility and service. "Be of the same mind," he told the Philippian church, "having the same love, being in full accord and of one mind. Do nothing from selfish ambition or conceit, but in humility regard others as better than yourselves. Let each of you look not to your own interests, but to the interests of others. Let the same mind be in you that was in Christ Jesus" (Phil. 2:2–5). In the Ephesian letter, a disciple of Paul set forth the same idea with this injunction: "Be subject to one another out of reverence for Christ" (5:21). Although it is not a particularly contemporary image, the idea was, I think, that Christian people were to be "equally yoked" together in love and service and mutuality because they were subject to the same benevolent Lord Jesus.

But it hasn't quite worked out that way. The issues of authority that were appropriately raised by the second and third generation of Christians soon became issues of power. Ambition and conceit struggled with service and humility, and the ethos of empires threatened the mind of Christ. With regard to women, the ethos of empire seems to have dominated, and one-half of God's people often have been forced into submission and servitude rather than being given the glorious *freedom to choose* humility and service. Indeed, in general ambition seems to have dominated service, and conceit to have silenced humility.

But not entirely. The gospel itself still sets off explosions in the lives of those who take it seriously. And those who try to extinguish the gospel light by putting it "under a bushel basket" and sitting on the basket to keep it covered will end up with scorched trousers! Although I would not argue that New Testament texts have not been *used and misused* to subdue those who were intended for mutual discipleship, I would suggest that the gospel itself continues "to bring good news to the oppressed, to bind up the broken-hearted, to proclaim liberty to the captives, and release to the prisoners; to proclaim the year of the Lord's favor" (Isa. 61:1–2) This was the passage that Jesus chose to proclaim in Nazareth, his "home synagogue" (Luke 4). As we say in homiletics, "it still preaches." Until men and women have reached the mutual discipleship envisioned by the reign of God, we need to hear it again and again.

Index of Ancient Sources

Index of Modern Authors